Exegetical Preaching

Spiros Zodhiates, Th.D.

52 Exegetical Outlines
Volume 4

Exegetical Preaching

Spiros Zodhiates, Th.D.

52 Exegetical Outlines
Volume 4

AMG
PUBLISHERS
Chattanooga, Tennessee

Exegetical Preaching
Volume Four

Softcover edition, 1998

ISBN 0–89957–488–2

Printed in the United States of America

03 02 01 00 99 98 –R– 6 5 4 3 2 1

CONTENTS

Contents

Contents

PREFACE

This book is a compilation of selected outlines which previously have been published in *Pulpit and Bible Study Helps,* a publication used by over 200,000 pastors and teachers of the Bible. These outlines are written to meet the need of those who follow the Lectionary, a system used by a number of churches. Each outline follows in order from Matthew to Revelation, one for every week of the year.

The unique features of this book include a key verse given for each outline, which is the focus of the entire passage the outline covers. In addition, an Index of Greek Words is provided listing each Greek word (transliterated) mentioned in the outlines along with a definition, the Scripture references where the word is found (if applicable), and the page number where each word occurs.

My prayer is that this volume of outlines will serve to be beneficial to those of you who are involved in teaching and preaching God's Word.

Spiros Zodhiates

A Shortcut Is the Devil's Tool

Key Verses: Matthew 4:1-11

I. **Christ Was Able to Successfully Confront the Devil**
   A. Although Jesus was both the Son of God and the Son of man, the devil and his followers seem to have attributed only humanity to Him. When the devil tempted Jesus, he treated Him as an exceptional human, but not as God in the flesh (Col. 2:9). Had he believed Jesus to be God which was demonstrated by the heavenly affirmation at His baptism, he would have left Him alone. It was because Jesus was without doubt "The Word . . . made flesh" (John 1:14) that He did not hesitate to have an encounter with the devil.
   B. We as believers, however, are not so led by the Spirit to be tempted by the devil. Rather, the devil is an adversary whom Peter compares to "a roaring lion, [who] walketh about, seeking whom he may devour" (1 Pet. 5:8). Therefore, Jesus teaches us to pray, "And lead us not into temptation, but deliver us from evil" (Matt. 6:13).

II. **The Devil Was Too Sure of Himself**
   A. Satan's pride was the basic cause of his downfall from heaven (Luke 10:18). He was not created as a devil but as an angel. He then rebelled against the supremacy of God (Is. 14:12–15; Ezek. 28:13–17; 1 Tim. 3:6).
   B. His activity in the world as "the prince of the power of the air" (Eph. 2:2) is limited (Job 1:12; Rev. 12:7–12).

In every confrontation with Jesus he was defeated (Matt. 4:1–11; Luke 11:14–22).

C. Twice Satan said to Jesus, "If thou be the Son of God" (Matt. 4:3, 6). The Greek word translated "if" is the suppositional conjunction *ei*, suggesting a condition which is merely hypothetical. It differs from another word for "if," *eán*, which indicates an objective possibility. Using the former shows that the devil did not really believe that Jesus was the Son of God.

III. The Devil Tried to Tempt Christ with Shortcuts

A. Part of fallen human nature is impatience, especially when our physical comforts or desires are concerned.

B. Thus, the devil thought he could convince Christ to change stones into bread after his forty-day fast. But Christ would not work a miracle for His mere comfort. We should likewise be wary of those who suggest constant miracles in order to bypass the hardships of life.

C. The devil's second temptation also involved a miraculous flaunting of supernatural power rather than waiting for His supernatural resurrection.

D. Lastly, he tried to tempt Christ with immediate rule over all the kingdoms of the world instead of waiting for His triumphant Second Coming.

E. The devil even tried to convince Jesus to avoid the cross as the means of our salvation (Matt. 16:21–23). Jesus called Peter "Satan" when he suggested such a thing, knowing that "without shedding of blood there is no forgiveness" (Heb. 9:22). We likewise must reject the devil's shortcuts.

Is Compassion an Option
or a Necessity?

Key Verses: Matt. 9:35—10:8

I. **What Aroused Jesus' Compassion?**
   A. Jesus was moved by the spiritual suffering of the people due to sin (Rom. 5:12). Their sin had caused a separation from God, or spiritual death. Thus, Jesus described them as "sheep having no shepherd" (Matt. 9:36).
   B. Along with spiritual death came physical death and many grievous diseases. Jesus also felt compassion for those with these physical afflictions. Therefore, from the very beginning of His ministry He combined both preaching and healing (Matt. 4:23–25; 9:35), providing an example for us to follow. We must treat both the physical and spiritual needs of the people to whom we minister.
   C. In doing so we must show the same compassion as that demonstrated by the Lord Jesus. The Greek word used to describe His sympathy in Matthew 9:36 is *esplagchnísthē*, derived from *splágchnon*, intestine or bowel. At that time the bowels were considered to be the seat of emotions, rather than the heart. It is not enough to be able to preach and witness; if we are to be like Christ, we must also have our inner being moved with compassion.
   D. Even believers in Christ are not exempt from sickness and death, but they can bear these things with full trust in God's providence. Christ continues to serve as our sympathetic high priest (Heb. 4:15) helping us

3

face death or any sickness or trial leading to it (Rom. 8:37–39). We will ultimately receive a new, resurrected body and at last be freed from the wages of sin (Rom. 6:23; 8:23; 1 Cor. 15:52–54).

II. Why Did Christ Feel So Moved?

A. Verse 36 says, "because they fainted." The graphic Greek verb employed is *eskulménoi* (Majority Text), the perfect passive participle of *skúllō*, literally meaning to skin, flay, or lacerate; it occurs in this form only here. The condition of humanity due to sin is truly a gruesome sight as perceived by our Lord (Rom. 3:23). We have been skinned by the thorny bushes and sharp rocks into which we, as sheep, happen to wander.

B. ". . . and were scattered abroad . . ." The Greek verb is *errimménoi*, the perfect passive participle of *rhíptō*, to throw or cast. Thus, the meaning is not merely "scattered abroad" but more violently being cast or thrown down.

C. ". . . as sheep having no shepherd." Finally, the sheep had been left totally defenseless. Their human leaders were false and unconcerned (John 10:12, 13). Jesus came, however, as the true Savior and Good Shepherd (John 10:1–5).

III. Mercy Is to Accompany Compassion

A. The Greek word "to have mercy" is *eleéō* from which *éleos*, mercy; *eleēmosúnē*, alms; *eleémōn*, merciful or charitable, are derived. Having mercy involves acting upon our compassion, *splagchnízomai* (Matt. 9:36). It is the outward manifestation of the inner feeling. Our Lord taught that both are necessary in Luke 11:41, which should really be translated, "but rather give as alms those things which you have inside you." Our good works then must emanate from a heart (or bowels) of concern, *eúsplagchnoi* (1 Pet. 3:8).

B. It is not an option for a believer in Christ to give alms (*eleēmosúnē*), but a necessity (Luke 12:33).

Who Receives God's Grace?

Key Verses: Matthew 11:25–30

I. **What Made Jesus Rejoice?**
  A. In Luke 10:21 (a parallel passage to Matt. 11:25) we are told, "In that hour Jesus rejoiced in spirit, and said, I thank thee, O Father, Lord of heaven and earth, that thou hast hid these things from the wise and prudent and hast revealed them unto babes: even so, Father; for so it seemed good in thy sight." This is the only recorded instance of Jesus rejoicing while praying to His Father.
  B. Was Jesus glad that the truth had been hidden "from the wise and prudent?"
  C. Or was He happy that it had been "revealed . . . unto babes"?
  D. Jesus never rejoiced in the lostness of men, but rather in their repentance (2 Pet. 3:9), even of the most lowly, the babes.

II. **How Is the Truth Hidden from the Wise?**
  A. The verb "hid" is *apékrupsas*, the aorist active of *apokrúptō* (*apó*, from, and *krúptō*, to hide). This hiding refers to those things which are known only to God and are purposely hidden from man's knowledge. No matter how clever one is, he will never find out these truths hidden from him by God. The truths of God which are *apókruphai*, hidden and unapproachable, cannot be discovered. They can only be revealed (*apokalúptō*) by God Himself. No human being, for exam-

ple, can possibly discover the mystery of the Trinity or the incarnation (1 Tim. 3:16). Jesus even spoke in parables to prevent the humanly wise from understanding God's truth (Matt. 13:10–17). Only to the humble is it "given unto you to know the mysteries of the kingdom of heaven" (Matt. 13:11).

B. The verb *krúptō* by itself indicates something that can be found by others (Matt. 25:18; John 19:38).

III. How Is Truth Given to Babes?

A. The two faculties which cannot understand God's purposely hidden mysteries (*apókrupha*) are wisdom and prudence, *sophós* and *sunetós* (Matt. 11:25). The verb "knoweth" (*epiginōskei*) in Matthew 11:27 really means to know by faith or supernaturally rather than to know by human means, an idea that would be expressed by the Greek verb *ginōskō* (in English we do not have an equivalent distinction). Thus, Jesus is teaching that God's truth comes through faith in the Son.

B. Babes are characterized by faith and trust rather than by confidence in themselves. That is why Jesus says we must "become as little children" in order to receive God's grace (Matt. 18:3). The cross is foolishness according to the wisdom of this world (1 Cor. 1:18). "But God hath chosen the foolish things of the world (the babes) to confound the wise . . ." (1 Cor. 1:27).

C. Realizing one's own utter helplessness is the first step to receiving the grace (or undeserved help) of God unto salvation. This is also indicated by the term "poor in spirit" being the first condition of blessedness, the state of acquiring God's nature (Matt. 5:3; 2 Pet. 1:4).

Love for God and Man

Key Verses: Matthew 22:34-46

I. **The Pharisees, Sadducees, and Scribes**
   A. The Pharisees
   1. Their origin:
      a) The name is derived from a Hebrew word meaning "separated."
      b) They were one of the most powerful sects among the Jews in the time of our Lord.
      c) The name does not occur before the New Testament period.
      d) Probably they were simply a continuation or development of the Assideans (the Pious) in the time of the Maccabees.
      e) They were always a minority group, and yet note how vociferous they were, just as some religious and political minorities are today. Under Herod they numbered something over 6,000.
   2. Their beliefs:
      a) They believed in the immortality of the soul and a future reward or punishment; the doctrine of a divine providence acting side by side with the free will of man.
      b) Their worst conflict with Jesus was the introduction of an oral tradition which they claimed descended from Moses and should carry the same authority as the written Law. The Sadducees, however, rejected these "laws."
      c) They became entangled in minute and subtle applications of the Law, which caused them to miss its spirit.

    d) Their religion degenerated into empty formalities which disturbed the people. They engaged in futile disputes over things such as what material the wick of the Sabbath lamp was made of, and whether or not it was permitted to eat an egg laid on the Sabbath day, etc.

B. The Sadducees

  1. The Sadducees, drawn mainly from the richer landowners, were a small party with a rationalistic turn of mind.

  2. They possessed limited influence with the people but they greatly influenced the high priests (Acts 5:17).

  3. They were worldly-minded and had only a superficial interest in religion.

  4. Their theology was in direct contradiction to the Pharisaic beliefs and was not popular.

    a) They denied the divinity and authority of the Law.

    b) They accepted the teachings of Moses only and not the later additions of the Old Testament.

    c) They denied the doctrine of the resurrection, believing that the soul dies with the body (Matt. 22:23). Consequent was their rejection of future rewards and punishments.

    d) They did not believe in angels or spirits (Acts 23:8).

    e) They believed in the absolute moral freedom of man, thus excluding the divine government of the world.

  5. They are not spoken of in the New Testament with the same bitterness as was applied to the Pharisees, yet they made common cause against Jesus in condemning Him to the cross.

  6. The sect disappeared after the first Christian century.

C. The Scribes
   1. They emerged during the exile, and Ezra was their leader and pattern (Ezra 7:6).
   2. They worked in great detail with the Law.
      a) They were the copyists of the Law.
      b) They engaged in its detailed teaching and were regarded as reliable teachers.
      c) They took great liberties with the text and made it void through their traditions (Mark 7:13).
   3. They were Jesus' determined and wily foes (Luke 5:30; 6:7; 10:25).
   4. The scribes formed a regularly organized college, into which members were admitted by special examination. The scribes and lawyers were one class.

II. **The Pharisees Rejoiced That Jesus Gagged Their Opponents, the Sadducees**
   A. The verb in Greek is *ephímosen*, meaning He muzzled them (also occurs in Matt. 22:34; Mark 1:25; 4:39; Luke 4:35; 1 Cor. 9:9; 1 Tim. 5:18; 1 Pet. 2:15). This concerned the subject of the resurrection and life in heaven (Matt. 22:23–33).
   B. They gathered together somewhere in the Temple where Jesus was.
   C. Mark 12:28 presents the Scribes as agreeing with Jesus' answer to the Sadducees and questioning Him further.
      1. The word used in Greek and translated "asked" in Mark 12:28 is *epērótēsen* from *eperōtáō* which Herodotus, in his *Histories,* mentions as consultations or questionings put before the oracle (1:53).
      2. This indicated that this scribe-lawyer looked at Jesus as related to deity who would possibly have the answer to the disputed question.
      3. Observe how close Jesus considered this scribe-lawyer to be to God's Kingdom (which only Mark records; see Mark 12:32–34.)

D. Luke, however, presents this lawyer as *ekpeirázōn* (Luke 10:25), tempting Jesus (*ekpeirázō* also occurs in Matt. 4:7; Luke 4:12, and in 1 Cor. 10:9).
   1. He wanted to use Jesus against the Sadducees, but at the same time he wanted to play the part of the tempting devil.
   2. What a subtle part an undecided, unredeemed person can play! He looks at Jesus as perhaps being God himself, but at the same time he does not hesitate to tempt God!

III. **The Scribe Asks the Question**
   A. "Which is the great commandment in the law?" (Matt. 22:36).
   B. "Which is the first commandment of all?" (Mark 12:28).
   C. Assuming Jesus is going to tell him which is the first commandment, he asks if by keeping it he could inherit eternal life (Luke 10:25).
      1. It was not an academic question for him.
      2. He wanted to inherit eternal life by doing something, which is a contradiction in terms. You do not do anything to inherit something. You just receive it. Such is the way of acquiring eternal life, receiving it by faith, for Jesus Christ did it all.

IV. **Jesus' Answer**
   A. Love God above everybody and everything else.
      1. But you cannot love someone you do not know.
      2. Receive Jesus and you will know God. "He that believeth on me hath everlasting life" (John 6:47), said Jesus. "The Father is in me, and I in him" (John 10:38).
   B. Then you can love your neighbor, not as merely a neighbor, but as you love yourself. Without God's love in you, you cannot in turn love your fellow man.

Why Does God Permit Suffering?

Key Verses: Mark 1:14–20

I. Introduction

A. All three evangelists, Matthew, Mark, and Luke, each begin their accounts of Jesus' public ministry with His return to Galilee, one year after He began his ministry both in Galilee and Judea.

B. The context of the passage is as follows:

1. Mark 1:14, 15 introduces the whole period of time from Jesus' arrival in Galilee to the time of Peter's confession about Christ's identity at Caesarea, Philipi (Matt. 16:15–19). What Jesus said and did during this period is recorded in Mark's first eight chapters. During this period, the Lord stayed in Galilee making Capernaum His home base.

2. Mark 1:16–35 contains some of the events of the first days of His public ministry.

II. The Reason Why Jesus Did Not Protect John the Baptist

A. Christ did not lack the power. The miracles He performed and His own resurrection proved that Christ could do anything.

B. What Christ did not do was not the result of impotence, but due to his wise choice.

1. At Bethesda, He chose to heal only one of many. This did not mean He loved one over the others. It takes more of God's grace to praise Him while suffering than to be delivered from suffering and sickness.

2. He could have instantly healed sick Lazarus as easily as raising him from the dead. He chose to do the humanly more difficult thing as a sign of what He was going to do to His own dead body.

3. He could have prevented Herod from arresting, imprisoning and killing John the Baptist, but He chose not to do it. He knew that God would be glorified more by John's death than by his continued life and ministry.

4. Herod did not exercise ultimate authority over John the Baptist. He was only performing what God permitted him to do. Mark 1:14 says, "Now after that John was put in prison. . . ." The Greek text uses the verb *paradothēnai*, the aorist infinitive passive of the verb *paradídōmi*, made up from the preposition *pará* denoting transition from one to another, and the verb *dídōmi*, to give. It means to deliver from hand to hand. It was power given from God's hand to Herod's. If it were not for such delivering, Herod could not have done a thing against John the Baptist. The aorist means that at a particular time determined by God Himself, this delivering was decided and executed by God. The passive voice indicates the decision was made by one other than John himself. This other was Herod directly, but God indirectly.

III. Suffering and Sickness Are Not Necessarily Due to Our Sins

A. All suffering, sickness and death are due to Adam's sin (Rom. 5:12).

B. Suffering and even death sometimes are brought about as a direct punishment for personal sin (Acts 5:1–11; 13:11).

C. Some of the greatest saints suffered more than sinners to demonstrate God's sufficiency through their bearing the necessary consequences of sinful humanity (Job, Paul, the Apostles; see 1 Cor. 4:9–13; 2 Cor. 11:22–33). That was God's choice for John the Baptist and has been for many believers over the centuries.

Jesus Commissions the Twelve

Key Verses: Mark 6:7-13

I. Jesus Chose Twelve Men to Be His Disciples
   A. He had selected them a year before (Mark 3:13–19)
   B. He allowed them to be with Him to see Him heal the sick, cast out demons, and demonstrate His authority in the spiritual realm by forgiving sins. They also saw Him refuse to do many miracles in Nazareth because of the unbelief of those who had known Him from childhood.
   C. After Jesus' second visit to Nazareth, "he went round about the villages, teaching" (Mark 6:6). Matthew 9:35–38 has a more detailed statement, including His healing of all manner of diseases and concern for the people's lost spiritual state. He then told His disciples, "The harvest truly is plenteous, but the laborers are few" (Matt. 9:37).
   D. It was in this context that the hour had come to officially send them forth (Mark 6:7).

II. Jesus Commissioned the Twelve to Assist in His Ministry
   A. All three Gospels mention this commissioning (Matt. 10:1, 5–15; Mark 6:7–11; Luke 9:1–6).
   B. They were told to "preach the kingdom of God, and to heal the sick" (Luke 9:2).
   C. Unlike the church's mission today, theirs was limited.
      1. They were charged to go to the lost sheep of Israel (Matt. 10:6) but not to the Gentiles or the Samaritans (Matt. 10:5).

15

2. They were not to take any provisions for their journey or settle in any location permanently (Mark 6:8, 10).

D. The disciples became Apostles in the strict sense of the word. Disciple (*mathētēs*) is a learner while an apostle is one sent out (*apóstolos*). As Christians we are both also, but in a general sense. The Apostles, on the other hand, were taught by Christ directly and sent by Him personally. He gave them a special message to propagate, "The kingdom of heaven is at hand," (Matt. 10:7) and special powers over the "unclean spirits" (Mark 6:7) for the casting out of demons and healing of the sick (Mark 6:13). Knowing how difficult this task would be, Jesus sent them out two by two.

III. Did the Apostles Accomplish Their Mission?

A. They preached in such a way that the result was repentance. "And they went out, and preached that men should repent" (Mark 6:12). The expression translated from Greek is "And when they went out, they preached so that people might repent." That should still be the goal of every sermon, to cause a needed change of mind, which is the meaning of repent (*metanoéō*).

B. With nothing but the words of Christ, they were amazed at the results they got. "And they cast out many devils . . ." (Mark 6:13). When the seventy whom the Lord later appointed returned following their mission (Luke 10:1), they were joyful, saying, ". . . Lord, even the devils are subject unto us through thy name" (Luke 10:17).

C. The apostles also healed the sick by rubbing them with oil (Mark 6:13). Elders are still commanded to do likewise in James 5:14. The verb used in both cases is *aleíphō*, to rub as contrasted with *chríō*, to anoint, which has a sacred meaning. James said, "*aleípsantes,*" having rubbed with oil, to pray, indicating the effectiveness of both medicine and prayer.

D. Their crowning achievement was that "his name was spread abroad" so that even "King Herod heard of him" (Mark 6:14). Glorifying Christ was the true goal of their mission, and all the other accomplishments were only the means to that end. The word "name" stands for all that a person is. What the apostles said and did manifested who Jesus Christ really was. Such is the disciple's task today, "Now then we are ambassadors for Christ" (2 Cor. 5:20). Are we living in such a way that we also will magnify His name?

The Responsibility That Follows Preaching

Key Verses: Mark 6:20-44

I. **The Apostles Had Successfully Completed Their Mission**
   A. They had preached the message of repentance, healed the sick, and cast out many devils (Mark 6:1, 12, 13).
   B. As a result, Jesus' name was made manifest in all the area (Mark 6:14).
   C. In fact, Herod was so disturbed by the report that he wondered whether John the Baptist, whom he had already beheaded, had risen from the dead and was active again.
   D. Mark, who adheres to the chronology of events, places the feeding of the 5,000 immediately after the Apostles' return, as if to show their continuing responsibility to the people.
   E. Indeed, they had physically healed several who were ill (Mark 6:13). How could they now ignore them?
   F. The miracle of the feeding of the 5,000 shows Jesus' continuing concern for the physical as well as spiritual welfare of those who follow Him.

II. **Our Bodies Are Not to Be Neglected**
   A. Jesus showed His concern for the health of the disciples themselves.
   B. After they had reported to Him of all that they had done and taught, He said to them: "Come ye yourselves apart into a desert place, and rest a while" (Mark 6:31). Then followed the explanation, "for there were many coming and going and they had no leisure so

much as to eat." The demands of their ministry were so great that they had no time even to eat.

C. The same thing had also happened earlier to His disciples and Himself when they had gathered in Peter's house in Capernaum. Mark 3:20 records: "And the multitude cometh together again, so that they could not so much as eat bread." This passage also indicates a lack of time available to eat.

D. Because of these pressures, Jesus instructed His busy disciples to get away to the desert where they would not be disturbed. The verb used for rest is *anapaúesthe*, which denotes rest in the midst of labor. This verb stands in contrast to *katapaúomai*, which means to rest from work entirely. The Lord did not want His disciples to be idle, but rather to have a change of scenery. Jesus knew the benefits of getting away from it all, long before the advent of modern psychology.

E. Jesus Himself went with them. Mark 6:33 makes this clear, "And the people saw them departing and many knew Him [Jesus]. . . ." In a similar manner, our rest can never be found outside of Jesus.

III. We Have a Responsibility Toward the Physical Needs of Those to Whom We Minister Spiritually

A. After Jesus and His disciples had taken a boat to go off by themselves, the crowds came after them on foot around the lake.

B. In spite of their need of physical rest, when the Lord saw the multitudes, He felt compassion for them. Do we feel a similar concern for those who seek our help at inconvenient times?

C. The Lord Jesus did not get back in the boat with His disciples to escape the crowd, but instead He began to teach them as if they were sheep without a shepherd (Mark 6:34).

D. The disciples realized that because they were in a desert, the people would not have an opportunity to find anything to eat. Therefore, they suggested the most convenient solution: "Send them away, that they may go into the country round about, and into the villages, and buy themselves bread: for they have nothing to eat" (Mark 6:36).

E. The most convenient solution to a problem, however, may not provide Christ the greatest glory.

F. Then Jesus commanded the disciples to do an impossible task, "Give ye them to eat" (Mark 6:37).

1. He knew they did not have sufficient food.

2. Jesus was able to provide the means whereby His command could be accomplished.

3. We should never say that anything is impossible with God. If we are in partnership with Him, we can accomplish all He desires of us.

G. By miraculously feeding the 5,000, Jesus showed that He was interested in their bodies as well as their souls.

H. How can we conceive of the joy the disciples experienced as they served all those people until they could eat no more? In Greek, the expression "they were filled" means they were fully satisfied, satiated. In the same way, when we satisfy the physical or spiritual needs of others, Jesus makes us full participants in His joy and that of those we serve. His provision fully satisfies. Can you imagine the consequences of the disciples' insistence that it cannot be done?

Responsibility and Opportunity

Key Verses: Mark 8:1-9

I. **Christ Among the Gentiles**
   A. Jesus crossed over into the borders of Tyre and Sidon
      (Matt. 15:21; Mark 7:24). He wanted to show that He
      was the incarnation of the God who so loved the
      world, not just the Jews, that He gave His only begot-
      ten Son that "whosoever," Jew or Gentile, believes,
      should not perish but have everlasting life (John 3:16).
   B. To the Syrophoenician woman He spoke of the sov-
      ereign choice by God through the Jews in the execu-
      tion of His plan of salvation and of the ages, yet He
      extended His power to heal her daughter (Matt.
      15:21–28; Mark 7:24–30).
   C. The Lord healed many among the Gentiles (Matt.
      15:29–31; Mark 7:31–37).
   D. He also fed the multitudes in the area of Decapolis
      (Matt 15:32–39; Mark 8:1–10).

II. **The Gentiles Were with Jesus Three Days**
   A. The Lord wanted their interest unaffected by material
      concerns. He did not feed them the first day, but at
      the end of three days.
   B. How many of us would spend three days with Jesus
      forgetting all about food?
   C. In both instances of feeding the multitudes (the 5,000
      Jewish men, women and children, [Matt. 14:13–21;
      Mark 6:30–44; Luke 9:10–17; John 6:1–14] and the

4,000 in Decapolis, possibly Jews and Gentiles or perhaps only Gentiles [Matt. 15:32–39; Mark 8:1–10]), it was Jesus who took the initiative for feeding them. He did not show indifference to the needs of the body.

1. With the 5,000 it was at the end of the day but with the 4,000 it was at the end of the three day period.

2. It was at this time that the opposition of the Pharisees and Sadducees became pronounced (Matt. 16:5–12; Mark 8:11–21). This was after a full demonstration for the needs of the body. Jesus healed and fed in spite of the knowledge He had that the leaders were going to resist Him spiritually.

3. His interest in the physical well-being of the people was the outcome of His compassion, (Matt. 15:32; Mark 8:2) and not for the purpose of causing them to believe.

   a) We must heal and feed out of compassion, not for the sake of proselytizing the people or promoting our point of view.

   b) Souls cannot be bought into the Kingdom of God. We must show compassion because we are Christ-like, not because we hope to coerce those we help to become what we are.

4. It is not Christ-like to just preach when those to whom we preach also need a ministry to the body in healing and feeding.

III. The Proximity of Tyre and Sidon to the Galilean Cities of Capernaum, Chorazin and Bethsaida

A. In these Jewish cities of Capernaum, Chorazin and Bethsaida, constituting a triangle, the Lord performed the greatest number of miracles.

B. But they did not believe as the vehement denunciation of the Lord showed (Matt. 11:20–24).

1. The Lord did not perform the largest number of His miracles among those who deserved them or who believed. He chose to do so among the Israelites to leave the chosen ones of Israel without excuse.
2. Jesus chose to demonstrate His power among the Gentiles of Tyre and Sidon to show them that His grace and power are extended among those who never thought they deserved them.
3. But at the same time, Jesus occasionally chose to withhold His power as with Nazareth, when He knew that they would continue in their disbelief.

C. Responsibility and opportunity are directly proportionate to each other. Those are more responsible who are given the greatest opportunity, such as the people who lived in Capernaum, Chorazin and Bethsaida.

Jesus Reveals the Coming Cross and His Resurrection

Key Verses: Mark 8:27–38

I. The Gospel of Mark Can Be Divided into Two Main Parts
   A. In Mark 1:14—8:26 Jesus proved Himself to be the Christ, God's Son, by His mighty teaching and deeds.
   B. Beginning at Mark 8:27, He started to teach about His passion and resurrection.

II. Why Did Jesus Ask His Disciples What the Multitudes Thought of Him?
   A. He wanted to show them the misunderstanding of the people.
      1. Despite His miracles, they thought of Him as a mere man: John the Baptist, Elijah, or one of the prophets (Mark 6:14, 15; 8:28). Matthew 16:13 adds "the Son of Man" ("Whom do men say that I, the Son of man, am?") This phrase emphasizes that His appearance among them was in His human form.
      2. The people were not expecting a suffering Messiah.
   B. He wanted to start preparing His disciples to accept the necessity of the cross and resurrection (Mark 8:31).

III. Peter Was the First to Proclaim That Jesus Was the Christ
   A. Peter's confession came in reply to Christ's next question, "But whom say ye that I am?" (Mark 8:29). The

phrasing indicates that He expected His disciples to have a more perceptive view of Him than did the multitudes.

B. After having been with Him constantly for two years, His disciples had seen His full humanity. At the same time, they had experienced His deity.

C. Thus Peter declared, "Thou art the Christ." The word *Christós* is from the verb *chríō*, to anoint. Matthew 16:16 adds "the Son of the living God." The definite article appears before the word "Son," as well as before "Christ," indicating that Jesus was the uniquely anointed One and the unique Son. There is also the definite article before the word "God," *toú Theoú*, which refers to God the Father. The addition of *toú zōntos*, the living One, means the One in whom there has always been life and who is, therefore, the dispenser of life. This addition stresses deity.

IV. Jesus Commanded the Disciples to Keep Silent

A. "And He charged them that they should tell no man of Him" (Mark 8:30). The Greek word that is translated "charged" is *epetímēsen,* which means to strictly forbid. In Matthew 16:20 the verb used is *diesteílato,* forbid or prohibit. What did He forbid them to tell? Matthew 16:20 clearly states, "that they should tell no man that He was Jesus the Christ." Why did Jesus not want His disciples to speak of His being the anointed Messiah? For one thing, He did not want the Jews to crown Him as their liberator from the Roman yoke. He knew that they would never change their preconceived notions about His ruling as Messiah until they saw the greatest of all signs, His resurrection from the dead. He therefore wanted His sacrificial ministry to be completed before His disciples revealed that He was the Christ.

B. In fact, it was not until after His resurrection that He began to be referred to as Christ Jesus rather than Jesus Christ—the reversal emphasizing the importance of His deity over His humanity (Acts 19:4; Rom. 3:24; 15:5; 1 Cor. 1:30, etc.).

C. The Lord's prohibition, however, was only temporary. The time would come when Jesus Himself would publicly announce His Messiahship. While Peter was warming himself in the high priest's yard after having denied Him, Jesus answered Caiaphas' question, "I adjure thee by the living God, that thou tell us whether thou be the Christ, the Son of God" (Matt. 26:63). "Jesus saith unto him, Thou has said: nevertheless I say unto you, Hereafter shall ye see the Son of man sitting on the right hand of power, and coming in the clouds of heaven" (Matt. 26:64). It was just before His crucifixion, then, that He stated in no uncertain terms that He was indeed the Savior.

V. **Jesus Taught Them the Inevitability of the Cross**

A. Although they perceived that Jesus was "the Christ, the Son of the living God," (Matt. 16:16), the disciples did not comprehend His mission.

B. Their lack of understanding is revealed by Peter who rebuked Jesus on hearing that He had to go to Jerusalem to suffer, die, and rise again on the third day (Matt. 16:21; Mark 8:31).

C. Jesus publicly declared His coming suffering (Mark 8:32). His subsequent rebuke of Peter, "Get thee behind me, Satan," silenced any further objections to His sacrificial death.

Jesus and the Demanding Disciples

Key Verses: Mark 10:35-45

I. God's Grace Is Offered to All
   A. God showers certain benevolence on all men. ". . . He maketh His sun to rise on the evil and on the good, and sendeth rain on the just and on the unjust" (Matt. 5:45).
   B. Other graces, however, must be sought: "Ask, and it shall be given you: seek, and ye shall find; knock, and it shall be opened unto you. For every one that asketh receiveth; and he that seeketh findeth; and to him that knocketh it shall be opened" (Matt. 7:7, 8). Salvation is among this latter category: "Him that cometh to me I will in no wise cast out" (John 6:37).

II. Jesus Gives Special Privileges to His Disciples
   A. Once we become the children of God by faith, we have direct access to His throne of grace (Rom. 5:2; Heb. 4:16; 10:19; 1 John 3:21, 22; 5:14).
   B. Even as children don't always know how much to ask of their parents, so we as Christ's disciples sometimes pray amiss.
   C. Wise parenting demands discretion in awarding our children their desires. Similarly, we must trust God to use wisdom in considering our requests.
   D. On the other hand, God wants us to come to Him with all our needs and to open our hearts to Him as His children.
   E. The Lord taught a basic principle of prayer in John 15:16: ". . . whatsoever ye shall ask of the Father in

my name, he may give it you." "In my name" places a limitation of the seemingly unlimited promise "whatsoever." The former phrase means that what we ask must agree with all that His name stands for and that it will help accomplish God's purpose in the world.

III. **What Precipitated the Request of James and John?**
   A. The Lord had just spoken the parable of the laborers (recorded only in Matt. 20:1–16). He then started for Jerusalem with His disciples, teaching them that there He was to suffer, die and rise on the third day (Matt. 20:17–19; Mark 10:32–34).
   B. Again His disciples preferred to ignore the unpleasant events facing them by focusing on their positions in the coming kingdom (Matt. 20:20, 21; Mark 10:35–37).
   C. Matthew mentions that Zebedee's wife came to Jesus to ask that her two sons, John and James, be installed, one on His right and the other on His left in His kingdom. Mark 10:37 records the sons making the request. First, however, they asked Jesus: "Master, we would that thou shouldest do for us whatsoever we shall desire" (Mark 10:35). Many modern-day disciples also pray with the same mentality.

IV. **What Answer Does Jesus Give?**
   A. Jesus did not mince words, "Ye know not what ye ask," (Matt. 20:22; Mark 10:38). The Greek word for "know" is *oídate*, referring to intuitive knowledge. What they were asking reflected that they were selfish disciples, just as people today who pray for personal prosperity. Paul calls those who thus seek for premature glory, "the enemies of the cross of Christ" (Phil. 3:18).
   B. In the parable Jesus had just told of the laborers (Matt. 20:1–16), He called the complaining laborer "friend"

(Matt. 20:13). But the Greek word used for friend is not *phílos*, a true friend, but *hétairos*, one who attaches himself to someone for personal gain. Jesus likewise called Judas *hétairos* (Matt. 26:50).

C. Jesus' response to James and John makes it abundantly clear that no disciple can achieve glory until he first participates in the work of Christ (Matt. 20:22, 23; Mark 10:38, 39).

Mercy Available at All Times

Key Verses: Mark 10:46-52

I. The Background of Jericho
   A. Jericho, in the days of Christ, was a stronghold surrounded by towers and castles with a great palace built by Archelaus, the son of Herod, in a very fertile oasis.
   B. It was a trade crossroads.
   C. There are numerous Old Testament references to Jericho (Josh. 2—6; 2 Sam. 10:5; 1 Kgs. 16:34; 2 Kgs. 2:4, 5; 25:5).
   D. Our Lord reached Jericho on the evening of the Thursday or on the morning of the Friday before the Passover.

II. No Contradiction in the Two Records
   A. Matthew 20:30 speaks of two blind men while Mark 10:46 and Luke 18:35 speak of only one.
   B. Luke 18:35 states that the Lord healed one blind man as He was coming nigh or entering Jericho.
   C. Matthew 20:29 states that Christ healed the blind man as He and His disciples were departing from Jericho.
   D. Bartimaeus may have cried out when our Lord entered Jericho and again when He left the town but was healed on his second appeal.
   E. These variations are indicative of the independence of the writers from each other.

III. He was Known by Name
   A. Bartimaeus means the son of Timaeus.

1. He was blind.
2. He was a beggar.
   a) The present participle *prosaítōn* in Mark 10:46 (also in John 9:8) from the preposition *prós*, toward, used here as an intensive, and *aitéō*, indicates persistent begging.
   b) He was always approaching the people so everybody knew him.

B. Because he was well-known, his case is well-recorded as an attestation of Christ's power.

IV. Bartimaeus Had a Distinct Insight into Christ's Dignity

A. Hearing a multitude pass by (Luke 18:36), Bartimaeus inquired what the noise was all about.
   1. He was informed that Jesus of Nazareth was passing by.
      a) The crowd apparently did not acclaim Christ for who He was.
      b) He was simply Jesus hailing from Nazareth.
   2. That designation did not speak well of Him since the general belief was that nothing good could come out of Nazareth (John 1:46).

B. Contrary to the general concept, Bartimaeus recognized who Jesus really was.
   1. He cried with a loud voice to be heard over the noise of the tumult.
      a) The verb used is *krázō* (Matt. 20:30; Mark 10:47) which is "shout with the intent to be heard."
      b) In Luke 18:38, the word is even stronger, *boáō*, an imitation of the sound produced, like the bellow of a *boús*, ox.
   2. He realized that the crowd might be wrong about Jesus.
   3. No individual today will seek Jesus if he does not first overcome the general rejection of Christ by the crowd.

4. The crowd was wrong, and Bartimaeus was right in his estimate of Christ.

V. He Went Directly to Jesus Through His Loud Voice

A. He could not see Jesus because he was blind.

B. But he used the faculty he had, his voice.

C. He did not seek an intermediary, either a disciple or a member of the crowd.

    1. We, too, should go to Christ directly.

    2. He will hear your cry of agony for mercy.

D. He called Jesus "Son of David" which was tantamount to recognizing Him as the expected Messiah.

VI. Have Mercy on Me

A. He was positive.

    1. He did not complain about his blindness.

    2. He realized his need.

B. He realized that Jesus could do for him what nobody else could.

C. What does "having mercy" mean?

    1. In Greek it is one verb, *eléeson*, which is derived from *éleos*, mercy, or God's alleviation for the consequences of sin.

    2. He recognized that his blindness was the consequence of man's sin in general and he suffered not necessarily because God singled him out, but because of the fall of man.

    3. Thus, in his request for the removal of the consequences of sin per se in his own life, he recognized also that he was a sinner (Rom. 5:12) and that Jesus could remove both sin and its consequences by His grace (*cháris*) in his particular case because it so pleased a sovereign God.

    4. This is demonstrated by Jesus' discernment of faith in his heart (Mark 10:52; Luke 18:42).

5. Not always, however, does the Lord necessarily remove the consequences of sin—such as a damaged
   liver because of a life of drunkenness—along with
   sin itself.
6. The restoration of the soul to God is immediate.
   Sometimes there is a restoration of the bodily marks
   of sin, but not always. This will take place for all
   believers as their corruptible bodies are replaced by
   incorruptible ones in the day of the resurrection
   (Rom. 8:23; 1 Cor. 15:53).

Life for Show or Service

Key Verses: Mark 12:38-44
Parallel Passages: Matt. 23:1-26; Luke 11:37-52;
20:45-47; 21:1-4

I. **Jesus Differentiated Between Two Kinds of People**
   A. First, there were those who loved to show off, as described in Mark 12:38–40.
   B. Secondly, there were those who loved to serve no matter how little they possessed (Mark 12:42).

II. **When and Why Was This Teaching Given by the Lord?**
   A. This teaching occurred on the Tuesday afternoon of Passion Week after Jesus had answered both the multitudes and His disciples (the full account is in Matt. 23:1–36 and a summary in Mark 12:38–44).
   B. Jesus first warned His disciples, "Beware of the scribes . . ." (Mark 12:38). The Greek expression for "beware" is *blépete*, see or perceive. His admonition was contrary to modern teaching about accepting people as they are. Jesus told His disciples to stay away from people who are not genuine, in order not to participate in their hypocrisy.

III. **Who Were the Show-Offs?**
   A. They were the scribes, or *grammateís*, which means the learned ones. To know is not evil in itself, but to be proud of it is worse than being ignorant.
   B. In particular, they studied the Law of God. After the return from the Exile, the duty of interpreting the Mosaic Law had fallen first to the priests, and later to a group called Scribes, who became professional students and

teachers of the Law. Due to this important task, it was tempting for them to assume the authority of God Himself. Even today pride lurks at every Bible student's desk and behind every pulpit. We, too, must be careful lest we become proud peddlers of God's Word.

IV. What Were the Characteristics of the Scribes?

A. Jesus first mentioned their dress. "Which love to go in long clothing" (Mark 12:38). The Greek word translated "in long clothing" is *stolaí*. *Stolé* (masc.) was a long, flowing robe reaching to the feet, which was worn by kings and priests, or other persons of rank and distinction (Mark 16:5; Luke 15:22; 20:46).

B. The scribes wished to be set apart in order to receive homage. Some salutations were abject prostration, and a slave might also kiss the sleeve or skirt of his lord's clothing to show respect. The Lord Jesus prohibited the seventy He sent out from engaging in such activity: "Salute no man by the way" (Luke 10:4). He said this to stress the urgency of proclaiming the Gospel.

C. The scribes, on the other hand, made a show of themselves by seeking "the chief seats in the synagogues, and the uppermost rooms at feasts" (Mark 12:39). They were more intent on drawing attention to their glory than God's. But "God is not a respecter of persons," and in Christ we are all one rank (Acts 10:34; Gal. 3:28).

D. The scribes were totally unworthy of the honor they demanded for themselves. They even took advantage of the poor by taking away the little food that widows had in their houses (Mark 12:40).

E. Lastly, they completed their shame by saying long prayers for show. By their actions they demonstrated their lack of love for either God or man. Because of their hypocrisy, Jesus said they would receive "greater damnation" (Mark 12:40).

V. **In Contrast Was the Widow Who Sacrificed**

    A. As Jesus sat opposite the treasury, He observed a widow put in a very small amount of money. He commented upon her gift to His disciples (Mark 12:42, 43).

    B. Even though her two coins would buy little, in comparison to what she had they were the greatest gift given that day. She had denied herself the necessities of life in order to give them to God. Only the Lord, however, saw the great worth of her sacrifice in contrast to the wealth others had given out of their plenty. They had their reward from men, but she received her commendation from God Himself (Mark 12:43).

The Birth of Jesus

Key Verses: Luke 2:1–20

I. **The Circumstances in the Births of John and Jesus**
   A. Both births were promised by the same angel, Gabriel (Luke 1:19, 26).
   B. When the angel appeared to Zecharias to tell him that Elizabeth was going to give birth to a son, the angel spoke to Zecharias differently than when the angel appeared to Joseph.
      1. He said to Zecharias, ". . . thy prayer is heard; and thy wife Elizabeth shall bear thee a son, and thou shalt call his name John" (Luke 1:13).
      2. Observe that the angel declared that this son who was going to be born was going to be his son, "shall bear thee a son."
   C. When the angel appeared to Joseph he said to him, "Joseph, thou son of David, fear not to take unto thee Mary thy wife: for that which is conceived in her is of the Holy Ghost. And she shall bring forth a son and thou shalt call his name Jesus: for he shall save his people from their sins" (Matt. 1:20, 21).
      1. Although he was given the responsibility of naming the child that was going to be born, the child was not proclaimed as his.
      2. The angel made it absolutely clear that John was the son of a human mother and a human father.
      3. He made it equally clear that Jesus was going to be the Son of a human mother, but not of a human father. He was conceived of the Holy Spirit.
   D. When John was born his birth was attended only by his father (Luke 1:57–67).

E. When Jesus was born His birth was attended by an angelic accompaniment and a heavenly proclamation of the significance of the newborn child (Luke 2:8).

II. Distinctives of the Birth of Jesus

A. As the announcements for the birth of John and Jesus were different, so were the actual births.

B. The birth of Jesus is placed in a reference to the history of the world. It was not an isolated incident of the birth of an ordinary child. It was an incident which was going to divide the history of the world into B.C., Before Christ, and A.D., Anno Domini, After Christ, the year of our Lord. No other birth of any child wrought such division in the history of the world.

C. When Mary and Joseph brought the child to the temple and presented Him to Symeon, the latter confirmed the universal impact of Jesus' birth upon the entire world, both Jews and Gentiles. He was declared to be "a light to lighten the Gentiles and the glory of thy people Israel" (Luke 2:32).

1. Note that in Matthew 1:21 the announcement of the angel to Joseph was: "And thou shalt call his name Jesus: for he shall save his people from their sins." That constitutes the primary purpose for His coming.

2. Luke, however, who wrote his gospel primarily to show the attitude of Jesus toward the Gentiles and the Gentiles' attitude toward Jesus, presents the fuller saying of Symeon as: "A light to lighten the Gentiles, and the glory of thy people Israel."

   a) He speaks here of God's full purpose in Christ Jesus.

   b) The Gentiles were going to be enlightened before Israel during the dispensation of Grace and

Israel's acceptance of Jesus was going to be postponed until after the great tribulation.

D. The Lord revealed this in His lament over Jerusalem described in Matthew 23:37–39 and Luke 13:34, 35.

1. He predicted that the day will come when the Jews also will say, "Blessed is he that cometh in the name of the Lord." The Jews have not yet said, "Blessed is he that hath come in the name of the Lord."

2. Romans 9—11 makes this very clear.

   a) Note Romans 11:11, "But through their fall [Israel's], salvation is come unto the Gentiles, for to provoke them to jealousy."

   b) Note also Romans 11:26 which declares: "And so all Israel shall be saved: as it is written. There shall come out of Zion the Deliverer, and shall turn away ungodliness from Jacob." This has not taken place yet, but it will take place as God's prophetic plan unfolds before the world.

E. Another distinctive of the birth of Jesus is that it took place in lowly circumstances in spite of the cosmic setting of His birth.

1. He was born in a manger and yet He was declared to be "the mighty one," *ho dunatós,* as the Greek text has it in Luke 1:49.

   a) "He hath showed strength with his arm; he hath scattered the proud in the imagination of their hearts."

   b) "He hath put down the mighty from their seats, and exalted them of low degree" (Luke 1:52).

2. He was going to be the heir of the throne, "He shall be great, and shall be called the Son of the Highest; and the Lord God shall give unto him the throne of his father David" (Luke 1:32).

3. All that, and yet He was born where none of us would ever wish to have any of our children born.

III. The Birth of Jesus in the Context of World History

A. Luke 2:1 does not provide superfluous information, but places Jesus in the context of world history: "And it came to pass in those days, that there went out a decree from Caesar Augustus, that all the world should be taxed."

B. God used the action of a pagan ruler to fulfill God's plan that Jesus should be born in Bethlehem of Judea.

IV. The Purpose of the Birth of Jesus

A. This is clearly expressed in verse 11, "There is born . . . a Savior."

B. He is a universal Savior and not only the Savior of the Jews.

V. The Earthly Conditions of the Birth of Jesus

A. "In those days . . . there went out a decree from Caesar Augustus. . . ."

1. Caesar Augustus was the first Roman emperor. His real name was Caius Octavius.
2. He was a great nephew of Julius Caesar.
3. He became the first emperor of the Roman Empire.
4. He bludgeoned the world into submission.
5. Jesus was born at this time in history when power was vested in one man. Yet the power of the greatest despot who ever lived on earth could not crush the emergence of a baby born in a stable.

B. The earthly condition of Mary and Joseph was entirely insignificant and yet their lives were affected by the decree of Caesar Augustus.

1. They went to Bethlehem totally unnoticed.
2. Was it all coincidence that during the rule of this despot a decree was issued for each one to register in his own ancestral town?
3. There was no coincidence here. It was all divinely appointed.

4. Matthew 1:22 declares very plainly that the mightiest man on earth can only act to fulfill God's will entirely unknown to him: "Now all this was done, that it might be fulfilled which was spoken of the Lord by the prophet, saying, Behold a virgin shall be with child and shall bring forth a son and they shall call his named Emmanuel, which being interpreted is, God with us."

C. The great fact of the birth of Jesus is described in Luke 2:6, 7.

   1. The word translated "inn" is *katáluma* (v. 7), which is merely an enclosure, simply walls where travelers might drive their cattle for the night, and in which sometimes there were apartments where they themselves rested; but no traveler could obtain food there.

      a) There was water, but no food, no host, no entertainment.

      b) Mary and Joseph could not even find room in the *katáluma,* or apartments where the travelers stayed, and so they went out where the animals were, and there they appropriated one of the stables.

      c) A lower birth could not be conceived.

   2. It must have been so lonely for Mary. One of the greatest moments in the life of a woman is when she gives birth to her firstborn. Someone usually wraps up the baby, but she had to do it herself.

D. Observe the activity of heaven the day Jesus was born. This is described in verses 8 to 20.

   1. An angel of the Lord stood by the shepherds, and the glory of the Lord shone round about them.

   2. It was nighttime.

   3. In all probability, these were temple shepherds, watching flocks intended for sacrifice.

   4. They did not expect this angelic visitation or such a pronouncement about the birth of the Savior. It came upon them suddenly.

    a) The angel did not appear in Caesar's palace to announce to him the birth of the child Jesus, but he came to humble shepherds.

    b) The shepherds were filled with fear at the sight of the angel.

E. Hope was born that day for a world in despair. From the human point of view it was one of the craziest expectations to believe that the birth of a child born in a manger would bring peace and freedom to men and women of all nations in every part of the world if they would only accept the purpose for which He came: to be their Savior.

Try Again

Key Verses: Luke 5:1–11

I. **The Scriptures Are Believable Because They Expose the Failures and Weaknesses of God's Greatest Heroes**

   A. A human author would have hidden David's hideous sins of adultery and murder (2 Sam. 11).

   B. The closest group of disciples of the Lord Jesus were Simon Peter, James and John. One would expect the choicest to be presented as faultless and successful at all times. However, they are the ones whose faults and failures are most pronounced.

     1. The Lord called Peter "Satan" (Matt. 16:23).

     2. The Lord rebuked James and John when they wanted heavenly fire to descend upon an inhospitable Samaritan village (Luke 9:54, 55).

     3. Who of His disciples failed to heal a desperately needy boy? The very three of the inner circle, Peter, James and John. They had the most glorious experience of being with Christ on the Mount of Transfiguration. They even saw Moses and Elijah, long dead. And yet they failed in the valley of human suffering (Matt. 17:1–21).

     4. At the very beginning of their ministry, the three closest to Jesus experienced failure in the very vocation in which they were experts, fishing (Luke 5:1–11).

       a) You would think that He would let them start with tremendous success at what they did best.

       b) But He did not. He wanted to show them right from the start that without Him they could do nothing (John 15:5).

5. The Lord permitted these same disciples, with others at the very end of His earthly life after His resurrection, to again experience failure at fishing (John 21:1–14). Who is singled out? Peter!

II. Failure Is Only a Prelude to Success

A. None of us can always succeed at what we do best.

B. If we did we would be proud and we would be impossible to live with.

C. We may succeed at what we set for our own goal, but this may not be God's goal for us.

D. If God has a different plan for us, there is one thing that He can do to cause us to change directions: cause us to fail in what we have chosen as best for our lives.

E. If God's choice and ours coincide, He may permit us success, but somehow He has a way of shattering self-confidence by permitting occasional failure. Instead of complaining at failure we must see God's hand of direction.

F. His choice of failure for us is His way of gaining our dependence upon His Word explicitly and unquestionably.

III. The Greatest Success Is Obedience to One Who Knows Best.

A. The disciples experienced disappointment at the beginning and end of their ministries.

B. But they ended with unimagined victory.

C. This victory was due to their obedience to Christ without argument.

D. Some battles we shall lose, but the presence of Christ guarantees victory.

E. Try again by carefully listening to Him who knows best. Do not give Him an argument that it is no use trying again.

Vertical and Horizontal Relationships

Key Verses: Luke 6:36–42

I. A Believer Is a Recipient of God's Love
  A. Man in his fallen state is basically selfish (Rom. 3:23).
    1. Man's love is for the purpose of accommodating himself, not for meeting the needs of others.
    2. For man to love unselfishly even as God loves, he must first appropriate God's love for him (John 3:16; 1 John 4:10–19).
  B. If man has truly received God's love vertically, he must show it both vertically toward God and horizontally toward his fellow man.

II. Love Must Be Demonstrated to All
  A. In our present earthly make-up as believers we possess the Spirit of God which is love, but there is still a remnant in us of our nature.
  B. Our philosophy is, I want to love you but I cannot completely disregard the consideration of what is in it for me, too.
    1. It is easier to love those who love us than those who do not (Luke 6:32).
    2. Loving those who love us is a reciprocation of love.
  C. Loving does not mean:
    1. Blindly accepting others.
    2. Irresponsibly accepting the harm they want to inflict upon God, us, and other innocent beings.
  D. Loving means:
    1. Properly evaluating others.

a) If they show love toward us we must recognize this.

b) If they show hatred we must recognize it as such.

2. A proper diagnosis of others equips us with knowledge to help others so that they may be healed of their illness and wrong attitudes.

3. It also means recognizing someone as a false prophet. We ought to recognize him as such, become cautionary for the sake of others, and redemptive insofar as he is concerned and those he was been able to mislead (Matt. 7:15).

III. If Our Vertical Relationship Is Right, Then Our Horizontal One Will Be Correct

A. In the area of judging others.

1. Do not misinterpret this commandment of our Lord.

a) Jesus does not encourage us to become self-centered and say, "I do not care what others think, say or do." We must care. Each of us is his brother's keeper.

b) It does not mean that we should allow others to do as they please if that adversely affects righteousness as we see it revealed in God's Word.

c) Examine Paul's statement in 1 Corinthians 13:7, "Love believeth all things." Does this mean even a falsehood? No. Verse 7 must be compatible with verse 6 which says, "Love rejoiceth, not in iniquity, but rejoiceth in the truth."

2. The Lord wants us to judge in the sense of evaluating. But He wants our evaluation of people and situations to be:

a) Correct. "Thou has rightly judged," the Lord said to Peter. The word for rightly in Greek is *orthós* which also means correctly or straight.

b) Just. To the hypocrites of His day, the Lord said ". . . judge ye not what is right?" The word for right is *díkaion* which means just, not from the perspective of personal benefit (Luke 12:56, 57).

c) Not superficially. The Lord said, "Judge not according to the appearance [*kat' ópsin*—according to what shows on the outside] but judge righteous judgment" (John 7:24). Go deep when you evaluate someone.

d) Not according to or after the flesh. Not by what or how it is going to affect my physical pleasure or my material gain (John 8:15). This is how Jesus contrasts man's judgment with His own which He called "true" *aléthés* (John 8:16), one that cannot lie. Our judgment must not be affected by personal material consideration.

3. As we judge we shall be judged.

a) The verb "judge not" in Luke 6:37 in Greek is *mé krínete* in the present active continuous. Let not that be your way of life.

b) "And ye shall not be judged." The verb here is in the aorist subjunctive passive which has the meaning of:

(1) A particular time when we will all be judged. It refers to the final judgment of believers and unbelievers (2 Cor. 5:10; James 2:12, 13). If we treated others with merciful judgment, we shall be judged with similar liberal merciful judgment.

(2) That we shall be judged by God is indicated by the passive voice. The subjunctive mood indicates that God's judgment is contingent; the rest of the verse tells us that it is contingent upon the kind of judgment we demonstrate on earth.

B. In the matter of condemning others.

1. "Condemn not [*katadikázete*]" (Luke 6:37). Our judgment, if incorrect, unjust, superficial, and from personal consideration, will result in condemnation instead of redemption.

2. Our diagnosis should lead to efforts to heal, not to bury.

3. Our present condemnation will result in God's condemnation of our shortcomings instead of their merciful considerations.

C. In the realm of forgiveness. "Forgive, and ye shall be forgiven" (Luke 6:37).

1. The verb here is not the common Greek word for "forgive" *aphíēmi*, but the verb *apolúō*, to set loose from oneself which involves "innocence" on the part of the one set loose.

2. We should try to do everything we can in order to:

   a) Declare the innocence of an innocent person. That means we set him or her loose or free of guilt.

   b) Cause the sinful to quit his sin and then to be proclaimed loosed from his sin.

   c) Not be merely condemning of the one who is truly sinful but to be redemptive. That is what the command *apolúete* means, "set loose from their sins," either by recognizing innocence or causing redemption.

Finding the Lost

Key Verses: Luke 15:1-10

I. **Sinners and Christ**
   A. What shocked Christ's contemporaries was that He
      habitually ate with and made Himself available to
      "sinners" and publicans, the hated tax collectors (Luke
      15:1, 2).
   B. When Jesus dined at the house of a Pharisee (Luke
      7:36–39), he said to Him, "This man, if he were a
      prophet, would have known who and what woman
      this is that toucheth him; for she is a sinner" (v. 39).
      In other words, a prophet worthy of his name should
      not allow a sinful woman like that to touch him.

II. **The Lord's Explanation of Why He Preferred Sinners**
   A. His answer was not given explicitly in a categorical
      manner.
   B. He answered in three parables:
      1. The parable of the lost sheep.
      2. The parable of the lost coin.
      3. The parable of the prodigal son.
   C. No explanation was required. Just an appeal to what
      any man would do in certain circumstances: "What
      man of you . . ." (Luke 15:4).
      1. God is not unlike man, whom He made in His
         image (Gen. 1:26).
      2. Man does not give up on what he once had and
         then lost. He goes after that which is lost.
      3. He concentrates his efforts to reclaim that which
         was once his.
      4. He does not renounce his right over that which is
         lost. The shepherd and the woman took the lost

sheep and the lost coin without asking anyone whether he or she could reclaim it.

5. In the first two instances the owners took the initiative because what was lost were not human beings.

6. The sheep and the coin represent what God has given those who belong to Him. His gifts to us are never ultimately lost. He reclaims them for us.

III. The Beatitudes in Luke 6:20–23 Explain the First Two Parables in Luke 15:1–10

A. The believer on this earth may voluntarily lose:

1. Riches. He is poor for the sake of the Son of Man (Luke 6:20, 22).

2. Food. Blessed are the hungering ones for ye shall be filled. There is plenty of food to come.

3. Laughter. Now you are crying, but the day is coming when you will laugh (Luke 6:21).

4. Esteem, fellowship, reputation (Luke 6:22). All these important parts of life you may lose, but you will find them in great abundance in heaven.

B. Whatever the believer loses temporarily he will find in heaven (Luke 6:23).

IV. The Cooperation of the Sheep and the Coin are Not Needed for Their Recovery

A. There is nothing the sheep or the coin can do to help in their recovery.

B. The Shepherd and the woman do all the work.

V. The Lost Man Must Take the Initiative to Return to His Father

A. God allows man to have his way. Choice of action is his prerogative.

1. The father was not to be blamed for the son's decision.

2. The father could not prevent the natural consequences of his son's choice (Rom. 6:23).

3. The time came when in the son's utter helplessness, he came under the conviction that the only hope of salvation was to return to his father. Had he not done that, he would not have been restored.

    a) That is the necessary state of spiritual helplessness found in Matthew 5:3 in the first beatitude. Poor in spirit means spiritually helpless!

    b) Recognition of one's helplessness is the first step toward restoration to the Father's house.

B. The father received the repentant son (John 6:37). God will receive you, too, if you will only come to Him through His Son who paid the penalty for your sin (Rom. 5:10, 11; 2 Cor. 5:18).

The Realities of Justice on Earth

Key Verses: Luke 18:1, 2

I. Jesus' Lesson for His Disciples

    A. Realize that it is the Lord Himself who is speaking. "He was telling them a parable" (Luke 18:1). The Greek verb is *élege*, the imperfect of *légō*, to speak. The noun related to this verb is *lógos*, or word, but it also means intelligence. The Lord Jesus in His pre-incarnate self-existence is called *ho Lógos*, meaning the Word (John 1:1), or intelligence expressed. The verb *élege* is in the imperfect to show that the lesson He was trying to convey was something He was constantly trying to get across and that this parable was simply one of the lessons on the subject.

    B. His lesson came as a result of a demand of the Pharisees as to when the kingdom of God would come (Luke 17:20). He informed them that the kingdom of God has two aspects: the present invisible reign of Christ in the hearts of individual believers, and the future visible outward kingdom (Luke 17:20, 21).

        1. The challenge of the present (Luke 18:1–8). As disciples of Christ, we need to know what is going to happen, but we must also roll up our sleeves and do what needs to be done here and now.

        2. The eschatological kingdom (Luke 17:22–37). The disciples were more prophetically minded than they were practically minded. They often wanted to know as much as possible about the future visible kingdom rather than about how God could use

them in the sinful town in which they lived (Luke 17:20, observe the "when").

II. Realities the Christian Must Face

A. The necessity to pray and not to faint, which is indicated by the Greek infinitive *deín* (translated "ought" in v. 1) of the verb *deí*, it is necessary, it needs. It is an impersonal verb which indicates necessity from the point of view of an order that exists that is sovereignty instituted.

B. Where you live as a disciple is not ideal. The ideal is yet to come.

C. Realize that the whole world you live in lies in the wicked one (1 John 5:19). Even the leaders of your government may be evil. "There was in a city a judge which feared not God, neither regarded man" (v. 2).

D. Through necessity, you must interact with the officials of your individual city. Possibly they are individuals who do not fear God or do not care about or show concern about their fellow humans.

III. Who Is a Judge?

A. A judge is an official of the town which in Greek is called *kritḗs*. In the narrow sense, it means one who sits to dispose justice (Matt. 5:25; Luke 12:58; 18:2, 6; Acts 18:15), but in a wider sense, it means a leader, a ruler, a chief as the Jews had to rule over them from Joshua to Samuel (Acts 13:20).

B. Originally, starting with Moses, judges were to declare the oracles of God and His divine precepts. They were to settle differences among the people and to give counsel (Ex. 18:13, 15, 16, 19, 20). Such were the officials originally instituted by God.

C. Jesus wants us to realize that many judges today:

1. Do not fear God. This characteristic of our present leaders is indicated by a participle. Jesus said of the

judge in this parable, "not fearing God" (*mḗ phoboú-menos*). The "not" is the relative and subjective negative *mḗ* as contrasted to the *ou* which is the objective and absolute negative not. Such leaders may not pronounce their personal viewpoints concerning God from the housetops, but they subjectively have no fear of God.

2. Make claims that justice can be executed by leaders who do not fear God. The present participle indicates that the unjust judge's personal belief about God was influencing the totality of his official behavior. Jesus teaches us that public decisions are affected by personal beliefs.

IV. The Fear of God

A. In the Old Testament "the fear of the Lord" is frequently a definition of piety (Deut. 4:10; 6:13) which prompts to obedient and loving service (Deut. 10:12). Whether fear is a desirable virtue or a phobia (derived from *phóbos*), depends on the reality and greatness of the object feared.

B. Of the judge it is said "not fearing the God" (*toú Theón*). There is a definite article before *Theón* indicating the one true God. The true God is the One spoken of (1 John 5:18–20) who, because of His greatness and holiness, is to be respected and worshiped (Ps. 111:9; 112:1).

C. The Apostle Paul summarizes the unjust and their actions described in Romans 3:9–17 by quoting Psalm 36:1 in verse 18 of that chapter, "There is no fear of God before their eyes." Man's relationship with God, or his lack of it, determines his treatment of men. "The fear of the Lord" was the rule by which the early Christians walked (Acts 9:35; 10:2; 2 Cor. 7:1; Phil. 2:12; 1 Pet. 1:17; 2:17; Rev. 14:7; 15:4; 19:5).

V. The Unjust Judge

A. The verb used to describe this leader's treatment of men is *entrepómenos,* the present participle middle voice of *entrépō,* to turn in upon oneself, from *en,* in, inward, and *trépō,* to turn. It means to become ashamed upon realizing something is wrong that could have been avoided or corrected. For example, it is used in Jesus' parable of the wicked vinedresser (Matt. 21:33–45; Mark 12:1–12; Luke 30:9–19). The statement is that when the ill-disposed farmers would see the son of the owner come, they would be ashamed of themselves as to the treatment they had extended to the previous messengers. The word *entrepómenos* actually means to consider the situation and to turn inward in serious reflection with a sense of personal shame. It is to be ashamed for one's personal indifference in a given situation (see Matt. 21:37; Mark 12:6 and Luke 20:13). In 2 Thessalonians 3:14 the same verb is used, but in this instance the translators correctly rendered the meaning by incorporating the idea of shame. Paul says that he who does not want to work should be made to feel ashamed (*entrapê*). The element of shame is incorporated in Titus 2:8 concerning the one who holds a view contrary to the sound word. But in Hebrews 12:9, as in Luke 18:2, 4, the translation is defective in that it ignores the element of self-shame. The unjust judge's philosophy was that he was not ashamed of the condition of his fellow humans and therefore showed no concern and extended no solutions to the problem.

B. The word *ánthrōpos,* man, for whom the judge had no regard, is used in the singular but in reality refers to all humanity. A person who is without the fear of God is without any consideration for others as the rich man was for the beggar Lazarus (Luke 16:19–21).

C. When the judge's philosophy of life was stated in general, the negative *mé* was used showing his disregard of man and his being unashamed of the tragic condition of his fellow humans. However, when he was personally challenged by the need of the widow, the relative and subjective not (*mē*) was changed to the objective and absolute negative *ou,* meaning not at all in any way. This was in reference to both his fear of God or shameful unconcern of his fellow human beings.

The Risen Christ and the Fearful Disciples

Key Verses: Luke 24:36–49

I. Variety of Appearances of the Risen Christ
   A. He appeared to the two disciples from Emmaus (Luke 24:13–25).
      1. He performed physical activities:
         a) He spoke with them.
         b) He walked with them.
         c) He ate with them.
      2. These physical activities were verified.
         a) Jesus had a body—His resurrection body.
         b) Yet there was no physical limitation to that body (Luke 24:31).
            (1) Jesus suddenly disappeared from their sight without walking away from them.
            (2) That is what our resurrection body will be like, having a form that is physical but not restricted to the laws of physical existence as we know them (Phil. 3:21).
   B. He had previously appeared to Mary Magdalene.
   C. He appeared individually to Peter and James (1 Cor. 15:5, 7).
   D. He appeared to all the disciples together (1 Cor. 15:7; Luke 24:36–49; John 20:19–23).

II. **Our New Birth Is Directly Related to Jesus' Resurrection (1 Pet. 1:3)**
   A. The only places that the verb *anagennáō*, to give new birth, is used is in 1 Peter 1:3, 23. First Peter 1:3:

"Blessed be the God and Father of our Lord Jesus Christ, which according to his abundant mercy hath begotten us again [*anagenēsas*] unto a lively hope by the resurrection of Jesus Christ from the dead" (See also 1 Pet. 1:23).

B. None of us can claim salvation if Jesus did not rise (1 Cor. 15:17).

III. **The Argument about the Resurrection Terminated by His Appearance**

 A. Some of the disciples may have said, "We won't believe it until we see Him ourselves."

 B. Jesus would not have left them in doubt concerning such a momentous event. A collective appearance allows greater credibility.

 C. He wanted to show them that His new resurrection body was real and yet not subject to physical limitations.

 D. Peter, to whom the Lord personally and individually appeared (Luke 24:34), must have been telling them all about it. But would they believe a denier (Matt. 26:69–75)?

 E. They had seen the Lord crucified with their own eyes, and even strong testimony to His Resurrection was hard to accept as fact.

IV. **The Disciples Were Afraid Before Christ's Appearance**

 A. They were afraid for their own safety.

  1. Since Christ's enemies put the disciples' Lord to death, they would not hesitate to kill them, too!

  2. They had ample evidence of His power, but they did not know about His will for them. Was it for them to die, too?

   a) When Christ did not intervene to stop His executioners it was not because He could not do it, but because He did not choose to do it.

    b) That is our position today as Christ's disciples. We know He can do anything, but His will in what He chooses for us is sovereign.

B. Man has an innate attachment to the known and visible.

    1. They would have preferred Jesus' preservation instead of His death and resurrection.

    2. The disciples were just as human as we are when we want to cling to life instead of having hope because of His resurrection (1 Pet. 1:3).

    3. They had not yet understood Christ's foreordained future.

        a) It was His will and purpose to die for our sins.

        b) It was His will that we should also die not for our sins but because of Adam's sin (Rom. 5:12).

        c) He died for our sins so that we may not have to die in our sins.

C. They were afraid because they thought that the preservation of our present body in its present mortal constitution is the most important thing God could do for us.

    1. We shall be afraid, too, if this is our philosophy of life.

    2. A change of one's philosophy of death to a view of it as a laying down of our mortal, corruptible bodies for future immortal, incorruptible and glorious ones, will bring peace to our life (Rom. 8:23; 1 Cor. 15:54; Phil. 3:21).

    3. Jesus, through His death, gained for us a present redemption for our souls and a delayed redemption for our bodies, demonstrated by His own bodily resurrection (Rom. 8:23).

Behold the Lamb of God

Key Verses: John 1:35-42

I. **John the Baptist Called Jesus "The Lamb of God" Twice**
   A. John called Jesus "The Lamb of God" when he spoke to the delegation of the Pharisees (John 1:24–29) who came to inquire who he (John) was.
      1. He told them that there stood among them One whom they knew not (v. 26). The verb used for "ye know not" is *ouk oídate* which refers not to experiential knowledge, but intuitive recognition. They were looking for a prophet or a king who would liberate them from the Roman yoke. The Pharisees thought that national slavery was their worst calamity, while in reality it was slavery to sin.
      2. They had no sense of sin, therefore no sense of the need of a Savior.
      3. "The Word became [*egéneto*] flesh" (John 1:14) in order that He might become the sacrificial Lamb of God.
      4. The most basic misunderstanding of the Jews was that they desired a king rather than a lamb to be sacrificed. They desired a liberator instead of one who would place Himself on the altar of sacrifice.
   B. The next day, in the presence of two of His disciples, Andrew and possibly John who wrote this Gospel, John again said, "Behold the Lamb of God" (John 1:35, 36).

II. **Why Is the Word "Lamb" Used in Referring to Jesus?**
   A. Although in English the word "lamb" occurs many times in the New Testament, the Greek *amnós* occurs only four times and is applied exclusively to our Lord.

1. The first time is found in John 1:29 in which he calls Jesus "the Lamb of God," adding "which taketh away the sin of the world."

2. The second time is the next day in John 1:36.

3. The third occurrence is found in Philip's explanation of Isaiah 53:7 and 8: "He was led as a sheep to the slaughter; and like a lamb [*amnós*] dumb [without a voice of protest] before his shearer [readying it for sacrifice], so opened he not his mouth: . . . for his life is taken from the earth" (Acts 8:32, 33). The verb for "is taken" is *aíretai*, the same verb used in John 1:29: "who taketh [*ho aírōn*] away the sin of the world."

4. The fourth occurrence of *amnós* is in 1 Peter 1:19, "But with the precious blood of Christ, as of a lamb without blemish and without spot."

B. The other Greek names translated as "lamb" are: *arēn*, in Luke 10:3 and *arníon*, the diminutive of *arēn*, which occurs in John 21:15 and refers to the believers over whom Peter was to watch. In Revelation our Lord is called *arníon* 27 times; but it is not the *amnós*, lamb readied for sacrifice, but the *arníon*, "lamb" **already sacrificed** and triumphant.

C. The Lord Jesus is called "lamb" (*amnós*) because it was necessary to demonstrate that the very purpose of His incarnation was to shed His blood for the sins of the world (Heb. 9:22; 1 Pet. 1:19–21; 1 John 1:7).

III. This Was the Fulfillment of God's Last Sacrifice

A. In Genesis 4, we have the lamb typified in the firstlings of the flock slain by Abel in sacrifice. The sacrifice, however, was only for himself.

B. In Genesis 22:8, Abraham said to Isaac, "God will provide Himself a lamb."

C. In Exodus 12, we have the lamb slain and its blood applied, the sacrifice being for the whole household.

D. In Isaiah 53:7 we have the identification of the lamb as a man.

E. In John 1:29 and 36, the Man is Jesus Christ, "the *Lógos* who became flesh" (John 1:14). His sacrifice avails for the whole world.

IV. Jesus's Sacrifice Unlimited in Time and Scope

A. John 1:29 says, ". . . who taketh away the sin of the world." The verb "who taketh" is the present participle *ho aírōn* which implies non-limitation in chronology. Although time-wise, Christ's sacrifice was in the future, yet it was present and continuous in its effect. The Lord said, "Your father Abraham rejoiced to see my day: and he saw it, and was glad" (John 8:56). The disciples did not have to wait till Jesus died in order to be saved. They were saved in anticipation even as we today and those in the future are saved in retrospect as a result of the exercise of saving faith.

B. Jesus paid the price for the sin of the whole world. He is the propitiation for our sins: and not for ours only, but also for the sins of the whole world" (1 John 2:2).

Christ, the True Manna from Heaven

Key Verses: John 6:35, 41–51

I. "I Am the Bread of Life."

  A. Thus Jesus spoke of His spiritual mission in the world. As God sent manna to the Israelites because of their physical necessity, so He sent Jesus for their spiritual salvation (Matt. 1:21). "For the bread of God is He which cometh down from heaven, and giveth life unto the world" (John 6:33). It is evident that the life the Lord speaks about is the spiritual life He came to give those who believe on Him and not mere sustenance of the body (John 6:27, 33, 39, 47). This spiritual life He offers is also referred to in the New Testament as eternal life (John 3:16; 6:40, 47, etc.) because it will last forever.

  B. "The Jews" who "murmured" (John 6:41) were those in the synagogue (John 6:59). They were probably not the same group that He had addressed in the open (John 6:22–40), but were local Jews (John 6:42) that had heard about His claim to be the bread of life (John 6:34). The verb in Greek means to manifest sullen discontent. It is in the imperfect, *egógguzon*, which indicates this fault-finding had been going on for some time.

  C. Their complaint was not merely about His claim to be the bread of life but also His assertion to have come down from heaven. What disturbed them was **who** He was and from **where** He came.

II. Who Is Jesus and from Where Did He Come?

A. Eight times in John's Gospel Jesus said who He was, each time to deepen our understanding of His provision for us.

1. "I am the bread of life" (John 6:35)—Bread is the basic sustenance for the physical life of man. Even so is Jesus for our spiritual life. Just as bread must pass through a process from the blade, to the ear, full corn, flour, dough, and baking, so also the life Jesus gives must be developed and molded, even fired, to make it complete and satisfying.

2. "I am the light of the world" (John 8:12). Jesus then expanded this statement to show that He came to guide His people into knowledge and right living: ". . . he that followeth me shall not walk in darkness, but shall have the light of life."

3. "Before Abraham was, I am" (John 8:58). The Greek says "before Abraham was brought to existence [*genésthai*], I am." Abraham was created, but Jesus was self-existent; He has always been (John 1:18).

4. "I am the door" (John 10:9) states that faith in Jesus is the only way of entrance into God's kingdom.

5. "I am the good shepherd" (John 10:11). Jesus is our personal protector just as the shepherd is of his sheep.

6. "I am the resurrection and the life" (John 11:25). Jesus raised us from spiritual death to spiritual life (Eph. 2:1). He also promised an incorruptible body (1 Cor. 15:52, 53) and a life far better than that of this earth (Phil. 1:21).

7. "I am the way, the truth and the life" (John 14:6). Jesus summed up the progression of the Christian life as it moves toward its completion in heaven.

8. "I am the vine" (John 15:5). Lastly, a Christian's usefulness comes from his indispensable union with Christ.

B. Jesus came from heaven, as is constantly stressed in the Gospel of John (3:13; 6:33, 38, 41, 42, 50, 51, 58).

1. The first man, Adam, and all his descendants are "of the earth, earthy" (1 Cor. 15:47). But Jesus is "the Lord from heaven" (1 Cor. 15:47), heavenly. He came from heaven, now resides in heaven, and will return from heaven someday to gather His own unto Himself (John 14:3; 1 Thess. 4:16).

2. His first coming was by means of a virgin impregnated by the Holy Spirit. This unique birth made Him both human and divine (Matt. 1:23; Luke 1:31, 35).

3. The verb "descend" is used eight times in John's Gospel in quite a variety of descriptive tenses.

a) The aorist participle *katabás*, the one who came, indicates a particular historical event and implies that Jesus existed before He came, unlike the rest of mankind (John 3:13; 6:41, 51, 58).

b) The use of the present participle, *katabaínōn*, the one coming (John 6:33, 50) indicates a continual coming. Just as the manna was provided daily to the Israelites in the wilderness, so spiritual life from Christ is continually being offered, "the bread which cometh down from heaven" (John 6:50). To benefit from Christ's provision, however, we must personally receive this grace (John 1:11, 12; 6:50).

C. In the perfect tense, *katabébēka*, "I have come down" (John 6:38), means that having come down, Jesus was then there. The Jews in the synagogue, as well as people today, had to deal with the fact of Jesus' presence. Will we murmur against Him, as they did, or will we receive Him as true manna from heaven?

The Resurrection and the Forgiveness of Sins

Key Verses: John 20:19-31

I. **Morning and Evening Appearances of Christ on Resurrection Day**

A. In the morning He appeared to Mary Magdalene (John 20:11–18) and the larger group of women (Matt. 28:9, 10; Luke 24:9, 10).

B. In the evening, the Lord walked through closed doors and entered the room where the disciples were (John 20:19).

C. In between those two appearances, the Lord appeared to Peter (Luke 24:34; 1 Cor. 15:5) and to the two disciples walking to Emmaus (Mark 16:12, 13; Luke 24:13–35).

D. That same evening Jesus appeared to the disciples gathered in the Upper Room; Thomas was not present (John 20:24).

E. After that there is an interval of a week. Jesus appeared again for the second time to the disciples, this time with Thomas being present (John 20:26–29).

F. There were actually ten disciples (Thomas and Judas were absent) on that first evening of the resurrection. Luke 24:9 tells us there were the eleven, but this was a collective designation for "the disciples." It also tells us that there were also others there: "unto the eleven, and to all the rest." We do not know how many others, but they must all have been believers. They had locked the door because they were afraid of the Jews (John 20:19). What brought them all together were the stories they had heard in the morning that Jesus had risen from the dead.

II. They Did Not at First Recognize Jesus in His Resurrection Body

A. There were occasions after His resurrection that He hid His identity, as He did at first contact with the disciples on the road to Emmaus (Luke 24:31).

B. Similarly, prior to His resurrection, the Lord could hide His identity, as when He went past His enemies and remained unrecognized (John 8:59).

III. He Greeted Them with Peace

A. He was in the room while the doors were still closed, a supernatural phenomenon. Imagine yourself being in that Upper Room. Would you be afraid? Anything outside of our common experiences troubles us.

B. The word "peace" in John's Gospel occurs only after chapter 14 when Jesus began to speak about His death (John 14:27). It is found now after His resurrection (John 20:19, 21, 26). Their peace was closely related to His death and resurrection. The acquisition of peace in one's heart is based on the crucifixion and resurrection of Jesus Christ. To Mary Magdalene He had said, "Why weepest thou?" (John 20:15) and to the group of women departing from the sepulcher, He said, "*Chaírete*" all hail, rejoice (Matt. 28:9). This was not a mere greeting as the translators have perceived it. Nor was His "peace be unto you." It was the joy and peace which was brought to the human heart as a result of the cross and that resurrection morning.

IV. He Showed Them Evidence of His Identity

A. ". . . he showed unto them His hands and His side . . ." (John 20:20). The scars were still there. It was as if He were saying to them that He was the same Jesus who shed His blood for you and the whole world (1 John 2:2) as the price for sin which is death (Heb. 2:9; 2 Cor. 5:13–21). Peace comes to man as a result of what Jesus Christ as the God-Man physically suffered on the cross in shedding His blood (1 John 1:7) and dying for us (2 Cor. 5:15). Note that Paul in 2 Corinthians 5:15 adds the fact and importance of His resurrection: ". . . but unto Him which died for them, and rose again." Blood, death, resurrection—that is what brought peace to individual hearts.

B. They rejoiced: As John 20:20 says, "Then were the disciples glad, . . ." There can be no true joy or gladness without the peace which Christ brings as a result of His shed blood, death and resurrection.

V. One Who Has Experienced Christ's Peace Must Share it in the Power of the Holy Spirit

A. For the second time that evening Jesus said to them, "Peace be unto you: as my Father hath sent me, even so send I you" (John 20:21). They already had His peace. Is this a higher grade of peace? Yes.

B. One can have enjoyment which brings so much joy that he is compelled to share it. Anything as good and joyous as Christ's peace becomes of greater value when shared than when simply acquired and kept for self.

C. Without the Holy Spirit one cannot adequately experience Christ's peace. This is why the Lord ". . . breathed on them and saith unto them, Receive ye the Holy Ghost" (John 20:22).

1. This caused the disciples to understand that all three Persons of the Trinity, the Father, Son and Holy Spirit, are involved in the process of man's salvation.

2. In the Greek, the definite article is not before the name "Holy Spirit." It is not "Receive ye **the** Holy Spirit," but "receive ye Holy Spirit." This was not

the same as the coming of the Holy Spirit as a personality entering into the world, initiating the dispensation of the Holy Spirit as Jesus promised on departure from earth consequent to His resurrection (John 14:17, 26; 15:26; 16:13). These passages refer to the personality of the Holy Spirit. He is referred to as the Comforter (the Paraclete) in John 16:7; *ekeínos*, He Himself, in verse 8; and *tó pneúma tēs alētheías*, the spirit of truth who was going to come to them after Christ's departure in verse 13.

3. In John 20:22, the Lord Jesus gave the Holy Spirit to the disciples for the power of witnessing and preaching Christ, which may be equated with the filling of God's Spirit (Luke 4:1; Acts 6:3, 5; 7:55; 11:24) for service. Without the power of the Holy Spirit none of us can effectively share God's message of peace unto salvation.

VI. The Forgiveness of Sins (John 20:23)

A. The disciples of Jesus were to expect results after Christ's empowerment, involving the Father, the Son, and the Holy Spirit in their witnessing of His peace.

B. There would be those who would confess Jesus as having risen from the dead (Rom. 10:9) and would be saved. Such needed to be told of what Christ actually did for them. He forgave them. No one else can forgive sins committed against God except Jesus Christ as God (Matt. 9:6; Mark 2:7). We, as disciples of Christ, must forgive sins committed against us (Matt. 6:12).

C. The verb *aphēte*, forgive, in John 20:23 is in the aorist subjunctive meaning once and not on a continuous basis. It refers to the confirmation that a person's sins have been removed by Jesus Christ and not to a continuous process of man (be he priest or anyone).

D. The verb *aphientai*, they are remitted, in John 20:23 is the present indicative passive of *aphiēmi*, forgive or remove. This is an assertion of fact. However, the passive voice indicates that the removal is done by God in Jesus Christ due to His death and resurrection (Rom. 10:9) and is a present, effectual removal of a repentant sinner's transgressions.

E. The contrary is also true if there is no sincere repentance and confession of sin resulting in the removal of sins by Christ. ". . . and whosoever [sins] ye retain [*kratēte*, in the aorist subjunctive as *aphēte*], they are retained" (*kekrátēntai*, perfect indicative passive showing that they had never been removed by Christ; not because of the deliberate and capricious exercise of the will of Christ's disciple, but because of the individual's lack of true repentance and confession of sin directly to Jesus Christ).

Can Anyone Become Righteous?

Key Verses: Romans 3:21-28

I. Man Has Been Proven Guilty
   A. Paul states unequivocally that man is responsible for his present fate of missing the mark God had set for him (Rom. 3:5–19). "They are all under sin" (Rom. 3:9); there are no exceptions (Rom. 3:23).
   B. Furthermore, the responsibility for sin is personal "for that all have sinned" even though everyone inherited this condition from Adam (Rom. 5:12).

II. The Only Way Sinful Man Can Be Saved Is Through Faith in Jesus Christ
   A. As Peter, "filled with the Holy Ghost," told the Jewish rulers and elders, "Neither is there salvation in any other: for there is none other name under heaven given among men, whereby we must be saved" (Acts 4:8, 12).
   B. Faith in Jesus Christ and His death for us is the only way we can obtain eternal life. In Romans 3:21, this whole process of salvation is called "the righteousness of God" and is mentioned seven times in Romans 1:17; 3:5, 21, 25, 26; 10:3 (twice); as well as in Matthew 6:33; 2 Corinthians 5:21; James 1:20; and 2 Peter 1:1. The means of the appropriation of the righteousness of God is "by faith of Jesus Christ" (3:22). Likewise in Romans 3:26 we read, "To declare, I say, at this time his righteousness: that he might be just, and the justifier of him which believeth in Jesus."

What is clear in both these passages is that the faith which we must exercise is associated with the person and work of Jesus Christ. As we believe, we are justified (see Gal. 2:16). This belief rests on the crucified (1 Cor. 2:2) and risen Christ (1 Cor. 15:17). It is aroused in man as he hears God's Word (Rom. 10:8, 17) and is energized by the Holy Spirit (John 16:7–11). On our part it involves acknowledging the truth about Jesus Christ and placing our entire dependence upon Him to save us from sin.

III. **This Faith Does Not Involve Our Keeping of the Law or the Performance of Works**

   A. "Without the law" (Rom. 3:21) does not mean that the law instituted by God does not exist. "Do we then make void the law through faith? God forbid: yea, we establish the law" (Rom. 3:31). Nothing that God did or said is ever invalidated. The law was never given in order to save us from sin but to confirm our sinfulness (Rom. 3:20; 4:15; 5:13–20; 7:5ff.; 1 Cor. 15:56; Gal. 3:19). The Jews could not and cannot be justified by the law of Moses (Acts 13:39). "But now," Paul says, "the righteousness [salvation] of God **without the law** is manifested . . ." (Rom. 3:21). The verb used is *pephanérotai*, the perfect indicative passive of *phaneróō*, "to manifest" and indicates a particular time of manifestation by God. In actuality God achieved salvation without the help of the law, which only confirmed sin but could not remove it. What the law could never do, it cannot do now for us, either. On the other hand, God's righteousness is "being witnessed by the law and the prophets" (Rom. 3:21). In other words, they do testify to the promise of God to provide a Savior.

   B. "Therefore we conclude that a man is justified by faith without the deeds of the law" (Rom. 3:28). Paul means not only "the deeds of the law," or duties prescribed by the Mosaic law, but any works (Rom. 3:20, 28). He uses the example of Abraham in Romans 4:2. Then in Romans 4:6 he speaks of the "blessedness" (*makarismón*, 2 Pet. 1:4; Matt. 5:2–11) of the man, unto whom God imputes righteousness without works (Rom. 4:6). Furthermore, how could a sinner do any good works when he is spiritually dead (Eph. 2:1, 8, 9)? Rather, he is first justified by God for the purpose of then being able to do good works (Eph. 2:10).

IV. **This Righteousness of God Is Available to All**

   A. Romans 3:22 declares: "Even [it would have been better to translate the particle *de* as 'and'] the righteousness of God which is by faith of Jesus Christ unto all and upon all them that believe; for there is no difference." The verb "is" in the phrase "is by faith" does not exist in Greek and should not have been used in English as correctly omitted by the NASB. The emphasis here is the "righteousness of God" (justifying the sinner) unto all. This phrase is *eis pántas*, meaning to each one no matter what one is, Jew or Gentile, free or slave, man or woman (Gal. 3:28). No one who is not justified can ever complain that he did not have the opportunity.

   B. God's justification, however, is not automatic. This truth is made clear by the phrase "upon [*epí*, indicating appropriation] all them that believe." Here is where the emphasis on faith belongs. Whoever believes is justified and never will be turned away (John 6:37). The Greek word for "all" is again *pántas*, "each one individually and all of them put together." The verb in Greek is *toús pisteúontas*, "the believing ones," the present participle of *pisteúō*, "to believe" and means those who are continuously believing. Once a person begins to believe, he is given a new nature which enables him to continue believing and begin performing works pleasing to God.

Baptized into Christ Jesus

Key Verses: Romans 6:3-11

I. **The Meaning of the Word "Baptize"**
   A. It means to dip, to immerse in water, as in the ordinance and practice of water baptism (Matt. 3:6, 11, 13; 28:19, etc.).
   B. Metaphorically, however, baptism is also used in the Bible with a broader meaning. For instance, in 1 Corinthians 10:2, it means "to identify with" as the Israelites "were all baptized into Moses in the cloud and in the sea." As they were enveloped by the cloud, they identified themselves with the character and purpose of Moses. Those who were baptized "into" (the Greek preposition *eis* is used here) repentance (Matt. 3:11), or remission of sins (Acts 2:38), or into John's baptism, identified themselves with that certain person or event.
   C. In Romans 6:3 and Galatians 3:27 the preposition *eis* is also used in reference to Christ, to be baptized **into** Christ. When the preposition is *epí*, "upon," as in Acts 2:38; and *en*, "in" as in Acts 10:48; the meaning is the same, to be identified with Christ.
   D. Baptism is also mentioned in the New Testament with reference to the Holy Spirit. As water is the agent in the physical baptism of the body, so the Holy Spirit is presented as the agent of the spiritual. Furthermore, a clear distinction is made between the two separate

baptisms (Matt. 3:11; Mark 1:8; Luke 3:16; John 1:33; Acts 1:5; 11:16; 1 Cor. 12:13).

II. What Is It That Identifies a Person with Jesus Christ or Makes Him a Member of Christ's Body?

A. A relationship with Jesus Christ is a spiritual union, and as such, it can only be accomplished by a spiritual transaction. In other words, no one can become a child of God by doing anything physical. On the contrary, we are saved by grace through faith, both aspects being spiritual in nature. God's grace changes the sinner to a saint by the means of faith. Baptism with water is simply a physical act, and thus is absolutely meaningless if one does not first believe on the Lord Jesus Christ (John 3:15–18, 36). Repentance, on the other hand, is spiritual and is associated with believing (Mark 1:15). Water baptism as a physical act should follow spiritual repentance or believing.

B. Whenever the words baptize or baptism occur, one must always examine the context to see whether physical or spiritual baptism is indicated.

III. Water and Spirit Baptism Symbolize the Death and Resurrection of Christ and the Believer

A. "Know ye not, that so many ["as many," *hósoi*] of us as were baptized into Jesus Christ were baptized into his death? Therefore we are buried with him by baptism into death: that like as Christ was raised up from the dead by the glory of the Father, even so we also should walk in newness of life . . . in the likeness of his resurrection" (Rom. 6:3–5).

B. Water baptism symbolizes the death and burial of the old man (Rom. 6:6). This is the death of the mind-set according to the flesh (Rom. 8:5–8). When we believe on the Lord Jesus Christ, He performs a spiritual miracle. He crucifies us and buries us together with Him.

Water baptism symbolizes that spiritual miracle but never causes it. Belief in Jesus gives us eternal life, which is our spiritual resurrection.

C. When the Holy Spirit perceives that the exercise of our faith is genuine and we have been truly born from above (John 3:3), then He attaches us to the Body of Christ. This permanent attachment is called the Holy Spirit baptism in 1 Corinthians 12:13, and it is something which Christ does for all genuine believers regardless of race, gender or social status.

God Did for Man What the Law Could Not Do

Key Verses: Romans 8:1-3

I. **The Advantage of Being in Christ (v. 1).**
   A. We are without a guilt sentence (*katákrima*, judgment of guilt).
   B. We walk not according to the flesh, but according to the Spirit. This is the believer's way of life. (The verb is in the present participle *peripatoúsin*, the walking ones).
   C. We are free from the dominance of sin and death (v. 2), the consciousness of our separation from God.

II. **These Advantages Were Not Granted Us by the Law (v. 3)**
   A. The Law in verse 3 does not mean what it means in verse 2 where it means dominance. Here it means both the written Law on the two tablets of stone and on man's heart by God Himself. This Law reveals the character of God, the Lawgiver, and reveals sin (Rom. 3:19, 20).
   B. This Law was impotent for it could not declare man guiltless, enabling him to walk according to the Spirit and freeing him from the dominance of sin and death (vv. 1, 2).
   C. We are free from the dominance of sin and death (v. 2), the consciousness of our separation from God.

III. **Why Is the Law Impotent?**
   A. It is without power to accomplish what Christ accomplishes in the life of the believer. The Law is impotent

in this particular matter, which is indicated by the expression *en hṓ*, in that which. The verb characterizing the Law is *ēsthénei*, the imperfect of *asthenéō*, to be without strength. The imperfect does not indicate occasional failure but constant failure. It was never meant to do what Christ did and does.

B. The Law's weakness was not in itself, but man's sinful nature here expressed as the flesh (*sárx*). The flesh, man's sinful nature, cannot be changed by the Law. It only points out the sinfulness of sin (Rom. 3:20). It could not and still cannot arrest sin (Rom. 7:9). When man's nature is changed through Christ, the Law's impotence becomes God's fulfillment in man, not only in that it shows how heinous sin is, but in that it arrests it and forgives it.

IV. **God's Provision (v. 3)**

A. "God" here stands for the Father. In the Greek it has the definite article in front of *Theós*; it is *ho Theós* which indicates the First Person of the Trinity, the Father.

B. God the Father sent His only Son: "Having sent His very own Son." The verb is *pémpsas*, the past participle of *pémpō*, to send, and is used transitively. Repeatedly, Jesus spoke of His having been sent by the Father (John 4:34; 5:23, 24, 30, 37; 6:38, 39, 44; 7:16, etc.) Here we have the recognition of two distinct eternal personalities (John 1:1, 14, 18) with a definite sending of the One within a historical context indicated by the past, *pémpsas*. Not only was Jesus sent by God the Father, but He came voluntarily (Eph. 5:25; 1 Tim. 1:15) indicating His equality with God the Father (John 5:18; Phil. 2:6).

C. Jesus took upon Himself a human body, yet different from our sinful flesh, "In the likeness of sinful flesh."

1. The eternal Son (John 1:18) or Word (*Lógos*), (John 1:1) became flesh (*sárx*) (John 1:14), but that flesh was without sin (Heb. 4:15 where the word *homoiótēs*, likeness, resemblance, is used which is akin to *homoíōma*, similitude, resemblance of in Romans 8:3). See the adverb *paraplēsíōs*, in a similar manner, in Hebrews 2:14. The flesh and blood of the incarnate Son of God were not sinful, and for this reason when the spirit of Jesus at death was delivered to the Father, His body did not see corruption (John 20:14; Acts 13:35; cf. Ps. 16:10).

2. Jesus being God (John 1:1; 10:30), became flesh (John 1:14; Heb. 2:14, 16; 5:7–9). He was sent, yet He came voluntarily. He was given a sinless body, yet He became (*egéneto*, the aorist indicative of *gínomai*, to become). Observe there is agreement between the past participle *pémpsas*, having sent of (Rom. 8:3), and *egéneto*, He became of (John 1:14).

3. Our flesh, as human flesh, is sinful unlike His (John 8:7; Rom. 5:12; Heb. 4:15).

V. The Purpose and Effectiveness of God's Provision

A. The eternal Son was clothed with human flesh in order to be able to die as the incarnate Son of God for our sins. "And for [*perí*, around, about, indicating with the genitive *hamartías*, of sin, the central point from around which His incarnation and death proceeded] sin." If it were not for man's sin (Rom. 5:12), it would not have been necessary for the eternal Son to become flesh (Phil. 2:6–8; note the use of *homoiōthénai*, to be made like in Heb. 2:17).

B. The incarnate Son condemned sin, that is, **the** sin, in its totality (1 John 2:2). The word for "condemned" is *katékrinen*, the past indicative of *katakrínō*, to bring final judgment. This is a compound verb from the intensive *katá*, and *krínō*, to judge, condemn (cf. Matt. 20:18; 27:3, indicating the finality of condemnation against Jesus as being parallel to the final condemnation of unbelieving sinners; Mark 16:16; 1 Cor. 11:32). Note the noun *katákrima*, utter sentence of condemnation, in Romans 8:1.

C. The means of the utter condemnation of sin are:

1. By the flesh. The Greek preposition *en* can have the meaning "by" in which case "the flesh" refers to Jesus' flesh. The utter condemnation of "the sin" of humanity came by the sacrifice of Jesus.

2. In the flesh. The same preposition *en* basically means "in," "in the flesh," which would refer to the supremacy of Christ's reign in man's spirit as well as in his flesh. No one can claim Christ's salvation and walk in the flesh (Rom. 8:1). The human flesh becomes sanctified in Christ (1 Thess. 4:3–5).

Watch Your Thinking

Key Verse: Romans 8:6

I. **Man's Ability to Think**
   A. Man differs from animals in that he can observe, think, and arrive at logical conclusions. He is endowed by God, his creator, with understanding. In the New Testament that is called *noús*, mind, the intellectual principle in man.
   B. The understanding of unbelievers is corrupt, not what God meant it to be. In Romans 1:28 Paul says, "And even as they did not like to retain God in their knowledge, God gave them over to a reprobate [*adókimon*, rejected, worthy of condemnation, useless, evil] mind." The unbeliever has a mindset that is evil. His thought processes are concentrated on the flesh and the gratification of his animalistic instincts.
   C. A synonym of *noús*, the mindset of man, is *phrónēma*, the result of the thought process. It is the crystallization of that on which man concentrates his mind. It is exclusively used in Romans 8:6, 7, 27. It means the result of the concentration of man's intellectual ability to think. The actual thought process is the word *phrónēsis*, prudence, thinking that leads to proper action in consideration of man's societal or horizontal responsibilities.

II. **Two Mindsets Are Possible**
   A. The mindset of unbelievers:
      1. Unbelievers are men of corrupt minds, *katephtharménoi*, utterly corrupted or depraved (in the mind) who also resist the truth and are unapproved in the faith (2 Tim. 3:8). See also Ephesians 4:17; Colossians 2:18; 1 Timothy 6:5; and Titus 1:15.

81

2. This mindset in Romans 8:6 is called "the mind [*phrónēma*], of the flesh." It is called that because the flesh and its gratification are what guide the thinking of unbelievers.

3. In Romans 8:5, Paul states that "those who are after [*katá*, according to] the flesh, do mind [*phronoúsin*, think constantly, the present of *phronéō*, think] the things of the flesh." This is their mindset. And this mindset is contrary to those who are after or according to the spirit, the sanctified spirit in their personalities as affected and shaped by the Holy Spirit. The same contrast is expressed in verse 6.

B. The mindset of believers:

1. Paul spoke of the law in his body warring against the law of his mind (*noús*) in Romans 7:23, and then in verse 25 he found himself serving the law of God with his mind.

2. He spoke of the mind of the believer as needing renewal (Eph. 4:23).

3. He spoke of the spiritual person as having the mind of Christ (1 Cor. 2:15, 16) in contrast to the natural man (psychic or *psuchikós*). In 1 Corinthians 2:14 *psuchikós* is translated "natural," in which case it is equivalent to *sarkikós*, carnal (1 Cor. 3:1).

III. The Fruit of the Mindset of the Flesh
A. Death. The verb "is" is implied.
B. Death here means spiritual death, or separation from God. He who constantly thinks of the flesh and how to gratify it is definitely separated from God.
C. Death stands in contrast to "life and peace."

IV. The Fruit of the Mindset of the Spirit
A. The spirit is the believer's spirit which is redeemed by Christ who freed the sinner (v. 2) from the prevalence of the law of sin.

B. "Life" is eternal or the life of God which Christ imparts into the believer (John 3:15, 16, 36; 10:10, 28).

C. "Peace" is the tranquillity Jesus Christ brings to the heart of the believer who seeks to please God in his spirit and thus has his flesh under control (John 14:27; 16:33; Rom. 14:17).

The Spirit Which Raised Christ from the Dead Will Also Raise Us

Key Verse: Romans 8:11

I. To What Spirit Is Paul Referring?

A. Here we do not have the Spirit of any particular personality of the Triune God, the Father, the Son, or the Holy Spirit, but simply and absolutely "the Spirit." It refers to the essence of God, for as Jesus stated, God is spirit (John 4:24). In Romans 8:9 the word "Spirit" occurs three times without the definite article before it. In verse 10 the contrast is between "the body," the material element of man, and "the spirit body," the spiritual element. This contrast is carried throughout this eighth chapter of Romans.

B. The theme is that our present salvation is only spiritual, while our future salvation will also include the redemption of our body (v. 23). While in the first seven chapters of Romans, the word "spirit" occurs only five times, in chapter 8, it occurs 20 times.

II. Who Raised Jesus from the Dead?

A. God the Father. "Now the God [*ho Theós*, God with the definite article referring to the Father; see John 1:1] of peace, that brought again from the dead our Lord Jesus . . ." (Heb. 13:20).

B. Jesus Christ raised His body from the grave by His Spirit. The flesh that He had as the incarnate son died, and His Spirit raised it up from the dead. This is clearly stated in Romans 6:4, where the Greek verb used is *egérthē*, the aorist passive of the deponent verb *egeíromai*, to rise. A deponent verb in Greek is one with the passive ending which is used in a middle sense, that is, I raise myself. Exactly the same form of the verb *egérthē* is translated in Matthew 8:15, in speaking of Peter's wife's mother, "and she arose" which is equivalent to "raised herself" (See also Matt. 9:25). In the case of the resurrection of Jesus Christ, *egérthē* would have been better translated not "is risen" but "He arose" or "He raised Himself" (Matt. 28:6, 7; Mark 16:6; Luke 24:6, 34). In Matthew 27:63 the deponent verb *egeíromai* is used and is translated, "I will rise again." This is the present indicative of the deponent verb and the correct translation is "I rise" or "I raise myself." The future of *egeíromai* is *egeroúmai*. Symbolically in predicting His resurrection, Jesus used the active voice of the verb in the future in John 2:19: ". . . Destroy this temple and in three days I will raise it up" (*egeirō̄*, the future of *egeírō*, "to raise it up," used transitively). Our conclusion is that if the Lord Jesus did not rise from the dead, He would not have been God" It was therefore the Spirit of Jesus Christ which raised His own body from the dead, and He indeed became the firstfruits of them that sleep—believers who are now indwelt by His Spirit (Rom. 8:9, 10). See Luke 18:33 where the verb *anastḗsetai*, the future middle of *anístēmi*, to rise, is used.

C. The Holy Spirit, as one of three personalities of the Triune God, raised Jesus from the dead. In Romans 8:11 it is used as "*tó Pneúma,*" the Spirit. This indicates particularly the personality of the Holy Spirit. It is used with the active transitive verb *toú egeírantos* (the one who raised Jesus) and *ho egeíras*, the one who raised Christ from the dead.

III. **The Spirit Which Raised Jesus from the Dead Indwells Us as Believers**

   A. There is no other power or personality which can raise anyone from the dead. Paul wants to remind us how great a power is the indwelling Holy Spirit (1 John 3:24; 4:4).

   B. Such indwelling of the spirit assures us of victory against the dead body (Rom. 8:10) and makes the ultimate redemption of the body a certainty (Rom. 8:23).

   C. His Spirit is alive and indwells; therefore, we can be more than conquerors in any circumstance (Rom. 8:37, 38).

IV. **He Will Revive Our Mortal Bodies**

   A. The verb translated "shall . . . quicken" is *zōopoiései*, the future indicative of *zōopoiéō*, to make alive.

   B. The Holy Spirit as well as the Spirit of the Father and of the son, Jesus Christ, makes us now spiritually alive by His cleansing us and dwelling within us. See the use of the word with its spiritual application in John 6:63; 1 Cor. 15:45; 2 Cor. 3:6.

   C. The Holy Spirit will also re-animate our present bodies by giving us resurrection bodies (John 5:21; Rom. 4:17). It is with this sense that the verb is used in Romans 8:11. Observe the word "also" (*kaí*, and, in addition). The translators, however, placed also before the verb "shall make alive" whereas in Greek it is after the verb *zōopoiései*. The verse should read "shall make alive also in addition our mortal bodies." The Spirit now lives in us. He has spiritually made us alive (Eph. 2:1, 2). But there is something more He will later do to our mortal bodies. He will raise them. (See 1 Cor. 6:14; 15:20, 23; 2 Cor. 4:14; Phil. 3:21; 1 Thess. 4:14.)

V. Who Will Raise Our Bodies?

A. God the Father: "For as the Father raiseth up the dead and quickeneth them . . ." (John 5:21).

B. God the Son, Jesus Christ: ". . . even so the Son quickeneth whom He will" (John 5:21; 6:39, 40, 44, 54). This is the resurrection especially of the believers at the coming of Christ for His saints (1 Thess. 4:13–18). There are two resurrections: the first for the righteous unto eternal life, and the second for unbelievers unto judgment (John 5:28, 29; Rev. 20:4–6).

C. In Romans 8:11 we have a grammatical structure that is not apparent in the translation: "But if the Spirit of him that raised up Jesus from the dead dwell in you." The word for "Spirit" is *Pnéuma*. But in Greek, Spirit is neuter, indicated by the article *tó*. Now when it comes to the next statement, "he that raised up Christ from the dead shall also quicken your mortal bodies by His Spirit that dwelleth in you," the phrase "he that raised up Christ" is in the masculine. This is referring to the Holy Spirit, not simply as the Spirit in the neuter, but also as a personality, the Holy Spirit. Again in the last statement, the reference is *tó*, the neuter, "the [Spirit] of his indwelling in you." We have here the Spirit (neuter) of the Father and of the Son and the Holy Spirit, a personality. A similar grammatical structure occurs in John 16:13, the literal translation of which is "But when he [that one, *ekeínos*, masculine single] the Spirit [neuter *tó pneúma*] of the truth. . . ."

VI. What Kind of Bodies Will the Believers Have at the Resurrection?

A. They will have incorruptibility and immortality. They will not separate from the spirit (1 Cor. 15:53).

B. Paul calls it a spiritual body, a body described in 1 Corinthians 15:42–54. It will be dominated by God's Spirit within us. We shall be like Jesus in His resurrection body (1 John 3:2; Phil. 3:21; Matt. 28:9; Luke 24:39, 41–43; John 20:19). Such a body is only for those who are indwelt by the Spirit. Then we shall be dominated by the Spirit.

We Must Live Without Obligation to Please the Flesh

Key Verse: Romans 8:12

I. Christian, It Is Your Life to Live
   A. When we believe Jesus Christ gives us life we still must determine how we are going to live that life. God does not conquer us. He frees us, enabling us to conform to His image. In verse 10, we are told that "the Spirit is life." But this freed spirit of ours functions in the inner environment of the flesh and the outer environment of the world.
   B. We as believers are debtors to the Spirit of God since He changed us. Paul recognized his indebtedness when he said in verse 2, "For the law of the Spirit of life in Christ Jesus hath made me free from the law of sin and death." As free believers, we have responsibilities: "Being then made free from sin, ye became the servants of righteousness" (Rom. 6:18). What is translated "ye became the servants" is the Greek verb *edoulṓthēte*, the aorist passive of *doulóō*, to make a slave (*doúlos*). The first thing that a believer must recognize is his new master. He is not free to do as he pleases, but to please his liberator. He is alive because of Christ's righteousness (Rom. 8:10). This slavery to Christ is not the satisfying or serving of the flesh. As Paul says in Galatians 5:1: ". . . be not entangled again with the yoke of bondage."
   C. As believers we owe nothing to the flesh, it was flesh and its propensity to sin which caused our fall in the

first place (Rom. 5:12; 8:10). We must view the flesh as our enemy, to whom we owe absolutely nothing.

II. Man's Propensity to Sin

A. It is possible for the believer to think himself indebted to the flesh since in this earthly life he is in the flesh (body). Let us never say, "After all, God gave me the desires of the flesh." They are the consequences of our disobedience to God. Our fleshly propensities are not God's gift. The expression "being in the flesh" (Rom. 7:5; 8:8) means "being by nature sinful." It is the opposite of "being in the Spirit." But in a sense, we as believers cannot escape being "in the flesh," that is, living in a body that is corrupt by nature (Gal. 2:20; 4:14).

B. We, being in the flesh (*en tē sarki*) or the body, must not live according to the flesh. The preposition *en*, in, conveys two ideas: being enslaved **by** the flesh or **in** the body, which is our present situation as believers. Being in the body, we must not live according to the flesh. This is indicated by the preposition *katá*, according to, which indicates voluntary conformity to the flesh, that is, sin. Although we are in the body, we, as believers, are not obligated (debtors, *opheilétai*, to live according to the flesh). It is to the Spirit of God within us to which we are debtors. The preposition *katá* is used in verses 1 and 4. Believers do not walk according to the flesh. There is a walk according to the flesh and a life according to the flesh (v. 12).

III. Sanctification Is Possible Only Because of Justification

A. Justification is what God does for us in Christ through faith (Rom. 5:1). He places us in the body of Christ (1 Cor. 12:13). It is the obtaining of the life of the Spirit while we are in the body (Rom. 8:10). It is Christ's reconciliation of man with God. Jesus Christ having paid by His blood the penalty of sin, can present us justified to God the Father (Rom. 5:2).

B. Sanctification is what we do with that life of God in us while we are in the body and in the world. The flesh or body is going to resist God's Spirit in us. The life of God in us results in a battle between the flesh and the Spirit.

C. But Christ washes our sins away and cleanses us from them (Heb. 1:3; 2 Pet. 1:9; 1 John 1:7). In 1 Corinthians 6:9, 10, Paul tells the Corinthian believers what some of them were before they were saved: fornicators, idolaters, adulterers, effeminate (passive homosexuals), those who sleep with men in homosexuality, covetous, thieves, drunkards, revilers, extortioners. In verse 11, he tells them they ceased to be that. How? "But ye are washed, but ye are sanctified, but ye are justified in the name of the Lord Jesus, and by the Spirit of our God." In English the voice of the Greek tenses are not clear and they need to be explained:

1. "Ye are washed" is *apeloúsathe*, aorist middle voice of *apoloúō*, to wash fully. The middle voice indicates that the individual himself takes part in the process. In Revelation 1:5 we read, ". . . Unto him [Jesus Christ] that loved us, and washed us from our sins in His own blood." The verb translated "washed" here is in the active voice, *loúsanti*, indicating that the work of cleansing or washing is by Jesus Christ. See also Ephesians 5:26 where the verb *katharízō*, to cleanse, is used. In 2 Corinthians 7:1, however, Paul admonishes the Corinthian believers to do some personal cleansing themselves when he says ". . . let us cleanse ourselves from all filthiness of the flesh and spirit, perfecting holiness in the fear of God."

2. The verb "ye are sanctified" is *hēgiásthēte*, the aorist indicative passive of *hagiázō*, to sanctify, make holy, set apart. It indicates the work of God in the believer's

life. There is a synonym of *hagiázō*, to set apart and maintain the cleanliness obtained by God. It is the verb *hagnízō*, to confirm purity or cleanliness. John, in writing of the believers now as having the hope of being one day in a position to see God as He is, says, "And every man that hath this hope in him purifieth himself, even as He is pure" (1 John 3:3). The verb here is in the active voice. It refers to the believer and to the work of maintaining the purity, the sanctification which he received from God's Spirit.

3. The verb "ye are justified" is *edikaiōthēte*. It is the aorist indicative passive of the verb *dikaióō*, to render just, justify, declare not guilty for one's sins because of what another did, and that is Jesus Christ. Never do we find any admonition in the New Testament that we as human beings can justify ourselves or improve on the work done by God in and through His Son Jesus Christ. The work of purification and sanctification pertains to our practical day-by-day living as we become God's co-workers, but not to our positional justification. It is this practical maintenance of our purity and holiness which Paul had in mind when he said in Romans 8:12 that we are not under obligation, indebted, to live according to the flesh (*katá sárka*), or to do anything to please the flesh. We are not in the flesh (*en sarki*), but in the Spirit (*en Pneúmati*) as stated in Romans 8:9.

Attention! What You Sow You Will Reap

Key Verse: Romans 8:13

I. **Before You Decide on a Way of Life, Stop to Think of the Already Declared Consequences**
   A. Our impulsive nature says "Do it." But before you do anything or choose your way of life, think of the consequences. They have been previously announced. Take what God says seriously.
   B. If Eve had taken seriously the warning of God, she would not have plunged humanity into the catastrophic consequences we now experience (see Gen. 1:1–13). God lets us choose, but He pre-sets the consequences of our choice.

II. **Can a True Believer Live According to the Flesh?**
   A. The total teaching of the New Testament gives a negative answer: "Whosoever is born of God doth not commit sin [*hamartían*, sin; *ou*, the absolute not; *poieí*, the present tense of *poiéō*, to do, which indicates a lifestyle] for his seed remaineth in him: and he cannot sin [on a regular basis] because he is born of God" (1 John 3:9). This statement is so explicit that there can be nothing to contradict it. A believer cannot claim to have God's seed in him and live a sinful life. There may be only an occasional sin for which there is always forgiveness upon repentance (1 John 2:1, 2).
   B. In Romans 8:13, Paul is not addressing the actual believers, but he proposes a hypothesis to show the absurdity of even imagining that a believer can live

93

according to the flesh. "If therefore" is how the verse begins in the Greek. The suppositional conjunction is *ei*, if, which is merely referring to a subjective possibility separate from all experience. This is one of the three conclusions indicated by *gár*, therefore. The other two are in verses 14 and 15 where *gár*, therefore, also occurs. If therefore you live according to the flesh, you sin continuously, Paul says. The obvious understood conclusion is that you cannot have the seed of God in you, for you cannot obey the flesh as a matter of course and be believers.

C. You cannot obey the flesh and not be experiencing progressive death. Not only are you not in the Spirit, not only does the Spirit not dwell in you, not only do you not have Christ's Spirit and you are none of His (vv. 9, 10), but you are going to suffer gradual death. The English translation "ye shall die" does not convey the Greek expression *méllete apothnéskein*. *Méllete* is the present indicative of *méllō*, you will, or you are in the process, and *apothnéskein* is the infinitive of the verb *apothnéskō*, to die off. If, therefore, you live (*zéte*, the subjunctive second person plural of *záō*, to live, to spend one's lifetime) according to the flesh, you are in the process of dying. Paul is not merely speaking of the end result of such a sinful lifestyle. He is not just stating "you shall die" as the translation has it, but you are dying and you will continue in that condition. If the English translation had stated it correctly, it would have been *méllete apothaneín*. The aorist infinitive *apothaneín* would have been used instead of the present infinitive *apothnéskein*. It is as if Paul is saying, "If you live according to the flesh, you do not have *zōé*, life, which results from righteousness." This is stated in verse 10.

III. A True Believer Mortifies the Deeds of the Body

A. There is a contrast here between the true believer and the deceived would-be believer who may think he is justified, but who lives in sin and is in the process of dying. The phrase that is understood is "but if you live according to the Spirit." Because of His indwelling presence, you will exercise that portion of your sanctification which is your responsibility as a believer, expressed as mortifying the deeds of the body.

B. What does to "mortify" mean? The Greek verb is *thanatoúte*, to mortify. In this context it means to subdue evil desires springing from our bodily desires. In verse 10, we were told that if Christ is in us, our body is still dead because of sin. Jesus Christ crucified our body together with Him, or rendered our "old man" dead (Rom. 6:6). Jesus Christ crucified our old man, but it is still in existence, showing its ugly face at every opportunity it can. But as true believers, we should follow the Spirit in us to destroy the deeds of the body. The difference between the false believer described in the first phrase of Romans 8:13 and the true believer is that the first does not recognize the overwhelming power of the presence of sin in his life which is killing him, while the believer spots all evil propensities or deeds of the body and overcomes them one by one.

C. This spiritual warfare is a constant process in the life of true believers. This is indicated by the tense and voice of the verb *thanatoúte* (present indicative active transitive). It could be translated "You constantly are killing the deeds of the body."

D. What are the deeds of the body? The word translated "deeds" is *práxeis*, from *prássō*, to do, and is used mostly of particular evil deeds (Luke 23:41; John 3:20; 5:29; Rom. 1:32; 2:1, 3; 7:19; 13:4; 2 Cor. 5:10;

12:21; Gal. 5:21). Therefore, Romans 8:13 is teaching that an unbeliever lives according to the flesh, and therefore he is dying and does not even realize it. The true believer, on the other hand, not only is in the Spirit (v. 9), but he subdues and overcomes the individual evil deeds of the body. Observe the triumphant note of Romans 8:37: "In all these things, we are more than conquerors." A true believer cannot be defeated by the evil deeds of his body. Observe also that the sinfulness of an unbeliever is characterized as living in the flesh (*sárx*, flesh), a term much stronger than *sṓma*, body. A believer lives in the body, but an unbeliever in the flesh.

E. What is the believer's weapon for mortifying the deeds of the body? It is the Holy spirit which indwells him, "Through or by the Spirit" (*Pneúmati*, the dative of *Pneúma*).

IV. Other Scriptures Indicating Our Part in the Process of Sanctification

A. In Romans 12:1, 2 we are told to present our bodies as a living sacrifice, holy, acceptable unto God, not to be conformed to the world, but be transformed by the renewing of our minds.

B. In 1 Corinthians 6:13, we are told that the body is not for fornication, but for the Lord; and the Lord for the body.

C. In 1 Corinthians 9:24, 25 we are told we must be temperate and exercise self-control in all things.

D. In 2 Corinthians 6:14 we are told not to be unequally yoked with unbelievers.

E. In 2 Corinthians 7:1 we are told to cleanse ourselves from all filthiness of the flesh and spirit (the body of the believer has both), perfecting or achieving holiness in the fear of God (See also Gal. 5:16, 24; Eph. 4:1, 17;

Phil. 2:12, 13; 3:16–20; Col. 3:1–10; 1 Thess. 4:1–5;
1 Tim. 6:11–16; 2 Tim. 2:19; Titus 2:11–13; Heb.
12:1; James 1:22–27; 4:7, 8; 1 Pet. 1:13; 2:11–25; 3:10,
11; 4:1, 2; 5:8, 9; 1 John 2:1–6; Rev. 22:12–15).

V. **Believers Shall Live: ". . . ye shall live."**
   A. The verb *zēsesthe* is in the future middle which means
      that your mortifying the deeds of the body will not
      detract from your present life (v. 10) any of its joy.
      The middle voice indicates that the believer's joy in
      his life in the spirit is in proportion to his effectiveness
      in the mortification of the deeds of the body.
   B. *Zēsesthe*, meaning you shall live, being in the future,
      stands in contrast to *apothnēskein* which is in the pre-
      sent continuous. The unbeliever who lives according
      to the flesh keeps on dying while the believer con-
      stantly mortifies the deeds of the body, enjoys his life
      in Christ and at the end, his enjoyment of life will be
      cumulatively precious. The believer will live in victory.

Do We Know How to Pray?

Key Verses: Romans 8:26, 27

I. **We Are Privileged to Pray, For We Recognize Ourselves as Children of God**
   A. In Romans 8:14, we are told that when we permit ourselves to be led by God's Spirit, we are "the sons of God." The word for sons is *huioí*, and implies in this passage that those are children who have not only experienced the new birth (John 1:12), but who are also consciously conforming to God's principles and will. The word "adoption" in verse 15 is *huiothesía*, being placed as a son. For us to realize that we are children (*tékna*, v. 16) of God takes the operation of the Holy Spirit. He does not stop with bringing us to salvation, but continues to work in us by making us conscious of our privileges and responsibilities to God.
   B. "The Spirit itself beareth witness with our spirit that we are the children of God:" (Rom. 8:16). The word for "children" here is *tékna*, from *tíktō*, "to give birth to." The first stage of our life as children of God then is the new birth (John 3:3).
   C. The Holy Spirit also gives us the consciousness that we can approach God as our Father (v. 15) and we are entitled to all that belongs to God our Father. We are not only heirs of God (v. 17) but also joint heirs with Christ, and so all that Christ has is ours in addition.

II. When We Pray, We May Act Proud of Our Inheritance and Utilize It Indiscriminately

A. The believer has so much power at his disposal that he may become reckless in how he uses it. Prayer is the means by which the believer makes use of his inherited spiritual power. The danger is that he may ask for too much and lose sight of God, the original provider, or he may ask for too little and think of God as inadequate. The believer may also ask for wrong things which may harm him more than help him.

B. Romans 8:26 begins with the adverb "likewise," *hōsaútōs*, which connects the previously mentioned idea of patience and hope to the work of the Holy Spirit. Indeed it is the Holy Spirit who helps us mature into sons as He assists us in praying for what we really need instead of praying for our own childish desires.

III. When We Pray, We Must Recognize That We Are Weak Without the Help of the Holy Spirit

A. "Likewise the Spirit also helpeth our infirmities . . ." (Rom. 8:26). The word for infirmities is *astheneías*, or lack of strength in all areas of life. When we pray, we must be possessed with both a sense of privilege and of weakness, physically and spiritually. We cannot command God when we pray or pretend to know what is best for us. Hence, we should always close our prayers "in the Name of the Lord," which is equivalent to "Thy will be done."

B. The verb translated "helps" in Greek is *sunantilambánetai*, found only here and in Luke 10:40 when Martha asked the Lord to make her sister Mary help her. The verb is composed of the conjunction *sún*, "together" and the compound *antilambánomai*. The latter is from *antí*, "in place of," and *lambánō*, "to receive." It means to help or take part with. In Classical Greek as well as Modern Greek, it also means "to grasp with the mind, perceive, apprehend" (Liddell and Scott, 1968). The meaning of perceiving precedes that of helping. The conjunction *sún*, "together," completes the verb *sunantilambánetai*. Thus, together the Holy Spirit and I first perceive my weakness and then the subsequent need for assistance from Him. In other words, I must cooperate with the Holy Spirit (Rom. 8:9) both in understanding my need of Him and in accepting His leading in my life (Rom. 8:14).

IV. The Ignorance of Our Real Needs as Believers Is Usually Demonstrated in Our Prayers (Rom. 8:26)

A. The verb "pray" is *proseuxómetha*, the future indicative of *proseúchomai*, "to pray to God." In each individual prayer we must wait and see if it is indeed God's will for us to be granted our petition. In fact, the Lord's humanity was also expressed in His prayer that the cup of the cross might pass away from Him (Matt. 26:39; Mark 14:36; Luke 22:42). How wonderfully His divinity was later shown when the Lord said to Peter, ". . . the cup which my Father hath given me, shall I not drink it?" (John 18:11).

B. The verb "we know not" in Greek is *oídamen*, (v. 26) which refers to intuitive knowledge. We cannot on our own, despite our saved condition, instinctively know for what we should pray.

C. In verse 27 the expression "maketh intercession" in Greek is *huperentugchánei*, found only here. It derives from the preposition *hupér*, "for, on behalf of," and the compound *entugchánō*, from the preposition *en*, "at, in, on, upon," and *tugchánō*, "to happen, to chance upon." Its meaning is that each time we pray about something, there appears the Holy Spirit joining together with us to plead for us in our weakness. At the same time that we pray, the Holy Spirit translates our earthly prayers "with groanings that cannot be uttered." "Groanings" is *stenagmoís*, used only here and in Acts 7:34. It is a sighing, usually of the oppressed (Acts 7:34), and is a feeling too deep for words. Why should the Spirit groan when we pray? Is it because we so often fail to pray for that which is God's eternal will but instead pray only in the context of the here and now? How the Holy Spirit sighs when He hears us pray!

God Kneels to No One

Key Verses: Romans 11:33-36

I. **Romans 9—11 Describes God's Dealings with Both Israel and the Gentiles**
   A. He sovereignly elected Israel.
      1. Jacob was chosen by God to rule over his older brother Esau through no merit of his own (Rom. 9:11–13).
      2. It was a choice based on God's grace, because both were children of wrath (Eph. 2:3).
      3. In fact, all mankind is under the penalty of physical and spiritual death (Rom. 5:12).
   B. He graciously elected the Gentiles
      1. Because of our sin, God determined to send His Son into the world, an act of great benevolence for the entire human race (Gen. 3:15).
      2. It was His plan that the Savior would be born of a virgin, a descendent of the seed of Jacob, or Israel as he was later called.
      3. Since only the Lord could devise an effective method of redeeming us, His actions should never be questioned (Rom. 9:19–29).

II. **God Can Never Be Accused of Sending Anyone to Hell Capriciously or Arbitrarily**
   A. In Romans 9:22 we read "vessels of wrath," which represent the unsaved, "fitted to destruction." These are the people who will experience ultimate estrangement from God. Now who fitted these vessels to destruction? Did they do it themselves because of their unbe-

lief, or did God arbitrarily reject them? In Greek the verb *katērtisména* is the perfect middle passive of *katartízō*, "to fit or to make fully ready." In Greek the form of the perfect passive is the same as that of the middle voice. If it is taken as passive, then it would mean that God fits them to destruction. If on the other hand, it be taken as middle, which the context here indicates, then it means that the people themselves are the ones who prepare themselves for this destruction. Nowhere do we read in Scripture that God places people in hell because He arbitrarily wants them there. To the contrary, we read in 2 Peter 3:9 that the Lord is ". . . not willing that any should perish, but that all should come to repentance" (See also 1 Tim. 2:4). Anybody who ends in hell can never claim that the Lord deliberately sent him there.

B. The Lord, however, is the only One who prepares anyone unto salvation. This is clearly indicated in Romans 9:23, "And that he might make known the riches of his glory on the vessels of mercy, which he had afore prepared unto glory." The Greek word translated "he had afore prepared" is *proētoímasen*, the active aorist indicative of *proetoimázō*, "to prepare ahead." This verb means that all vessels of mercy are actively prepared by God Himself. Thus no one can ever claim that his presence in heaven is deserved, but rather it is totally due to God's mercy (Rom. 9:16).

III. God's Mercy Causes Paul to Break Forth into a Doxology

A. "O the depth of the riches . . ." (Rom. 11:33). God's mercy makes rich all those who by faith become the recipients of it (Rom. 9:23; Eph. 1:7, 18; 2:7; 3:16; Phil. 4:19; Col. 1:27; 2:2). The richest man on earth is really the one on whom God has shown such abundant mercy.

B. ". . . of the wisdom and knowledge of God!" (Rom. 11:33). God also makes us wise. The word here is *sophía*, "wisdom, the ability of the right relationship with God." In such a way God makes us knowledge-able, when His knowledge becomes ours.

C. Because of these attributes, we know God cannot err in our regard (Rom. 11:33). We must trust in His wisdom since His judgments are unsearchable; the word *anexereúnēta*, found only here, is "inscrutable." It is as impossible to evaluate God's judgments as it is for a little child to understand his parents' decisions. We must simply trust and obey them.

D. "For who hath known the mind of the Lord?" (Rom. 11:34). The verb here is *égnō*, the aorist indicative of *ginōskō*, "to know experientially." The translation should be "for who knew the mind of the Lord?" with the aorist tense referring to the time at which God made the decision.

IV. **Man Can Never Act as God's Counselor**

A. ". . . or who hath been his counselor?" (Rom. 11:34; see also Is. 40:12–14; Job 15:8; Jer. 23:18). These passages show that God never asked advice when He created the world and, similarly does not require it concerning the final disposition of all things. The word for counselor, *súmboulos*, occurs only here in the New Testament, and it refers to the legislative rather than the executive will of God, or the very planning of all things. The things planned refer back to Paul's previous statement (Rom. 11:26) that in the future a multitude of Jews would come to accept Jesus as their Messiah.

B. In the meantime (Rom. 11:25), a partial blindness has come to the Jews so that the Gentiles will be given an equal opportunity to be saved.

V. We Cannot Expect Interest without Having Made a Prior Investment

A. "Or who hath first given to him, and it shall be recompensed unto him again?" (Rom. 11:35; cf. Job 35:7; 41:11).

B. As his final argument, Paul points out the obvious fact that we have made no contribution whatsoever to God and, therefore, deserve nothing from Him in return. The verb *proédōken*, is derived from *pró*, "ahead" and *dídōmi*, "give." Who made the original deposit? It was not man, but the Creator. As the original investor in us, God is the only One who has the right to judge what ultimately happens to His investment. "Or who hath first given to Him. . . ." The, *autō̃*, "Him," in the first clause refers to God. The second *autō̃*, "and it shall be recompensed unto him again?" refers to man. In other words, we have no claim on God whatsoever. He is entirely His own boss.

Future Salvation

Key Verses: Romans 13:11–14

I. **Our Present Salvation Is Only Partial**
   A. What is salvation?
      1. In English the word derives from the Latin *slavare*, to save, and *salus*, health, help.
      2. In Greek the word is *sōtería* and its cognates, *sōzō*, to save; *sōtér*, savior. It means cure, recovery, redemption, remedy, rescue, welfare which implies the action or result.
      3. In the New Testament, the deliverance from sin is salvation. This is to be found only in and through Christ (Acts 4:12).
   B. The word "salvation" is mentioned by Jesus only once (Luke 19:9).
   C. Our Lord, however, used "save" and kindred terms to indicate His primary purpose in coming to earth (Matt. 18:11; 20:28; Luke 4:18; 9:56).
   D. Salvation as found in the Pauline Epistles:
      1. Is through faith (Eph. 2:8).
      2. Is not be means of the law or works (Rom. 3:20; Gal. 2:16; Eph. 2:9).
      3. Is provided as the free gift of God, manifesting His grace toward the undeserving sinner who by the God-given grace of faith trusts in the righteousness of Christ who has redeemed him by His death and justified him by His resurrection (Rom. 5:11; 2 Cor. 5:18–21; Gal. 4:5–7; Eph. 1:13; Col. 1:20).
   E. The Lord Jesus redeems our soul-spirit but leaves it in the same mortal, corruptible body. This present body

of ours does not cease to be either mortal (Rom. 6:12; 8:11; 2 Cor. 4:11; 5:4) or corruptible (1 Cor. 15:53, 54). We as Christians continue to deteriorate physically and ultimately die.

1. Salvation or redemption was secured on the cross through the death of the Lord Jesus Christ (Is. 53; Rom. 3:25; 1 Cor. 6:19, 20; 7:23; Eph. 1:7; Heb. 9:15). He paid the price required for man's salvation or redemption with His blood (Mark 10:45; Gal. 3:13). This spiritual salvation is only "the firstfruits of the Spirit" realized by the believer here and now (Rom. 8:23), but since we continue to be in the body and on this earth our salvation is only partial.

2. There is, however, a future salvation, that of our present bodies being changed into incorruptible and immortal ones (Rom. 8:23; 1 Cor. 15:54, 55). These resurrection bodies of ours will live in a wonderful new environment. Such will be the new (*kainē*, qualitatively new) earth and heaven (Rom. 8:20–22; Rev. 21:1). This new body free from disease, death, and corruptibility was also made possible through Christ's death (Matt. 8:17), but its realization is in the future. This future salvation of the body and restoration of the fallen universe is a source of great encouragement to the now persecuted and suffering believers.

II. Paul Was Writing to Persecuted, Suffering Believers

A. They lived under one of the worst rulers the world has known, Nero.

B. Yet they were told to obey their secular rulers (Rom. 13:1, 2). If it were not for God's sovereign will, there could have been no Nero.

III. They Were to Evaluate Their Time

A. He begins verse 11 by saying, "And that. . . ." What he meant is, "Think of it this way."

B. "Knowing the time." The verb "knowing" is *eidótes*, from *oída*, to know intuitively. Being saved believers, they could intuitively see much more and beyond their current circumstances. That is something an unbeliever cannot do. What is translated "time" is *kairón*, season, opportune time, in contrast to *chrónos*, which is chronological time without any consideration as to the opportunity provided. See an opportunity in your current adversity.

C. The opportunity was not to allow adversity to put them into a spiritual sleep, thinking that because Nero reigned, God was dead and they could slumber.

IV. The Danger of Falling Asleep in Inactivity Imposed by Persecution

A. They apparently had fallen asleep insofar as the demonstration of their faith is concerned. The person who is asleep is under the false impression of safety when everything around him is afire. "Let's just lie low through it all" provided a false sense of security.

B. Paul stresses that knowing what you know as believers, you should awake from such a slumber. To spend your life in a spiritually comatose condition is not living. To hide your light lest Nero kill you is worse than death. It is better to die standing up and fighting the good fight of faith than to pass away sleeping and unnoticed by God and men.

V. The Salvation of the Body After Death

A. The Christian should be unafraid of death because it is then that the delayed salvation of the body is nearer than when he believed. The lesson then is that we should not be afraid of death which may result from our living righteously and witnessing courageously for Christ, since death draws us closer to the hour of the redemption of our bodies.

B. Death for the believer then becomes gain since his life is Christ (Phil. 1:21).

How to Be Fully Charismatic

Key Verses: 1 Corinthians 1:1–9

I. **Who Is Charismatic?**
  A. The word "charismatic" is derived from the Greek word *chárisma,* free gift, which in turn is derived from *cháris,* grace. Grace is a benevolent action on the part of God. Man does not deserve this. It does not simply mean to let someone go "scot-free" in spite of his action deserving punishment.
  B. In the New Testament man is never presented as dispensing grace. It is always the grace of God or of our Lord Jesus Christ (Luke 1:30; 2:40, 52; John 1:14, 16, 17; Acts 11:23; 14:3, 26; 15:11, 40; Rom. 1:5; 3:24; 5:15; 12:3, 6; 16:20, 24, etc.). Why? Because when God dispenses His grace, He does not simply declare the sinner free but also delivers him from the power of sin, although not from its presence or consequences. To experience the grace of God means to be saved, to be declared just before God (Rom. 5:1, 2) and to be made just or to have God's righteousness become ours (2 Cor. 5:21). We are saved from sin and are attached to God by becoming His children (John 1:12).
  C. In order to be saved we must possess God's grace in Jesus Christ, brought into our hearts through the Holy Spirit. This miraculous transaction of grace occurs only as all three personalities of the Godhead are activated in our life.
    1. God the Father receives the saved sinner. "By whom [Jesus] also we have access [*prosagōgḗ,* ushering unto

God the Father] by faith into the grace wherein we stand, and rejoice in hope of the glory of God" (Rom. 5:2).

2. This grace is possible because of the work of Christ on the cross in paying for the penalty of our sin. It is "through our Lord Jesus Christ" (Rom. 5:1).

3. Without the Holy Spirit we could not even conclude that God loves us, ". . . because the love of God is shed abroad in our hearts by the Holy Ghost, which is given unto us" (Rom. 5:5).

D. As a result, we are said to have all the *charísmata*, or gifts of the Holy Spirit. In Greek, words ending in *–ma* indicate the result of an action. *Cháris* is grace; the result of grace is *chárisma*, no matter what form in which that grace desires to manifest itself. Therefore any believer, by virtue of the possession of God's grace through Jesus Christ by the Holy Spirit, is fully charismatic. That indwelling grace can manifest itself in any result that the Triune God, from whom grace originates, sovereignly desires.

II. The Gifts of the Holy Spirit

A. We often speak of the gifts of the Holy Spirit, but in reality we are not correct in designating them as "spiritual gifts."

B. In 1 Corinthians 12:1 we do not have the right to take *tôn pneumatikôn* to mean "spiritual gifts" or "the gifts of the Spirit." In the Greek there is no noun following the adjective *pneumatikôn*, "spiritual ones," which in this instance is used as an adjectival noun. It means spiritual matters instead of material matters, and refers rather to things concerning our spiritual welfare.

C. If you notice carefully, 1 Corinthians 12:3–7, all three personalities of the Triune God are mentioned: the Holy Spirit in verses 3, 4, 7; the Lord in verse 5; and God the Father in verse 6—the administrator of the gifts of the Holy Spirit.

D. How many *charísmata* are there?

1. In 1 Corinthians 12:8–10 we have the word of wisdom, the word of knowledge, faith, gifts of healings (in Greek it is plural), the workings (plural in Greek) of miracles, prophecy, discernings (plural in Greek) of spirits, kinds or families (in Greek *génē*) of languages, and the interpretation of languages.

2. In addition, in 1 Corinthians 12:28–30 we have apostles, prophets, teachers, helps, and administrations. In Romans 12:6–21 we read, "Having then gifts [*charísmata*] differing according to the grace that is given to us whether prophecy . . . or ministry . . . teaching . . . exhortation . . . giving . . . ruling . . . mercy . . . love," etc. In Ephesians 4:11 we have evangelists and pastors added. But as Paul says, these and any other gifts (*charísmata*) are according to the grace (*cháris*) given unto us (Rom. 12:6). In other words, when God gives us His grace He also gives us the potential of any of the results of His grace as He sees they are needed for the benefit of others, not for our own exaltation and distinction from other Christians (1 Cor. 12:7 [*sumphéron*, mutually profit]).

3. He divides these gifts as He will (1 Cor. 12:11).

4. He is absolutely sovereign both in the granting of His grace and in the results of His grace.

III. **How Not to Lack In Any Gift**

A. In 1 Corinthians 1:7 Paul says: "So that ye come behind in no gift [*charísmati*]. . . ." How could these Corinthian Christians be said not to lack (*husteréomai*) in any gift? The answer is in 1 Corinthians 1:4: "I thank my God always on your behalf for the grace of God which is given you by Jesus Christ."

B. To have the grace of God is to be made rich: "That in everything ye are enriched by Him, in all utterance, and in all knowledge" (1 Cor. 1:5).

C. The greatest enrichment is that the Christian has the blessed hope (Titus 2:13). "That ye come behind in no gift waiting for the coming of our Lord Jesus Christ."

D. The greatest gift is the fellowship that a believer can have with the Lord Jesus Christ (1 Cor. 1:9).

Is the Cross Foolishness?

Key Verses: 1 Corinthians 1:18-31

I. The Logic of the Cross
A. What is translated as "the preaching" (v. 18) in Greek is *ho lógos*, the word. That is the same word we find in John 1:1, "In the beginning was the word," etc. *Lógos* means intelligence and its expression. Thus the first declaration Paul makes is that there is nothing illogical or irrational about either Christ or the cross.
B. We humans recognize that since there evil people exist, a method must be devised to punish them. The behaviorist system of punishments and rewards is certainly considered an intelligent system, and its practice is acclaimed as part of civilized humanity. It is wise not to let the evil person go unpunished and unchecked, and not to leave the good and benevolent unrewarded. When God does the same thing, why call it foolishness?
C. The cross indicates the necessary punishment for man's sins. "This is a faithful saying, and worthy of all acceptation, that Christ Jesus came into the world to save sinners (1 Tim. 1:15). The cross is the punishment that God planned and demanded for man's sin.
D. Why did God choose the cross as a means of man's salvation?
1. Because He had already established the system of sacrificing animals whose blood was sprinkled by the high priest on the mercy seat in the Holy of Holies on the Day of Atonement. It was an objective sacrifice to satisfy God's justice, that sin may not go unpunished. But this propitiation (*hilasmós*,

114

1 John 2:2; 4:10; or *hilastérion*, Rom. 3:25) was an objective provision for pity or mercy. However, the blood of animals could not convert the sinner. Even the high priest himself had to sprinkle animal blood for his own sins (Heb. 5:3). The high priest, through his sacrifice, could not change the sinner to make him a friend of God, because he was a sinner himself.

2. In order to satisfy God's justice it was necessary to have blood shed, for "without shedding of blood is no remission" of sin (Heb. 9:22). But this sacrifice and sprinkling of blood had to be done by the high priest every year on the Day of Atonement (Lev. 16:15, 16, 21, 22).

3. It was not the blood of animals, but of the sinless Son of God who became flesh with blood to shed once and for all for our sins, and thus satisfy forever the justice of a Holy God. Because he continued to sin, man could not be reconciled to a Holy God on his own. But the blood of Jesus did more than satisfy God's justice. It takes away man's sin from him. It cleanses the hearts of those who believe (1 John 1:7, 9) and implants in them God's nature or His righteousness (2 Cor. 5:21; 2 Pet. 1:4). Now man, being cleansed and made holy, can be separated not only away from sin but unto a Holy God. This is called atonement or reconciliation, *katallagé* in Greek, and it involves a radical change in the sinner (Rom. 5:11; 11:15; 2 Cor. 5:18, 19). The verb "to reconcile," *katallássō*, occurs in Romans 5:10; 2 Corinthians 5:18–20. We are reconciled to a Holy God by the death of God's sinless Son called the Word (*Lógos*) who became man so that He could die for us. Romans 5:11 states: ". . . but we also joy in God through our Lord Jesus

Christ, by whom we have now received the atonement." This atonement took place through Christ's death as Romans 5:10 clearly states: ". . . we were reconciled to God by the death of His Son." Both the shedding of His blood when blood and water came forth as His side was pierced (John 19:34) and His death (John 19:30, 33) were represented at the cross. The cross therefore means the shedding of the blood and the death of Christ, and that, Paul declares, is logical and it is worth preaching. It is "the word of the cross." To God it made sense because it was the only perfect sacrifice that could be made the way that He had foreordained to punish sin and to liberate man from sin who, as a changed, saved, and converted person, could then be brought to God. God, the Creator of man, knew that he can never be what God created him to be unless man is in fellowship with Himself. Therefore this plan of salvation through the cross and the ensuing resurrection was the only way whereby this restoration of man could be accomplished. It is logical, not illogical.

II. **Man's View of the Logic of the Cross Depends on His Condition**
   A. To them who perish it is foolishness.
   B. To them who are saved, it is the power of God.
   C. There are only two classes of people—the lost and the saved. It makes absolutely no difference what race or social class one belongs to.

III. **The Lost—Who Are They?**
   A. To be lost means not to be found where one or someone ought to be. In the three parables of Luke 15, we see a sheep that was lost because it was not in the fold, a coin that was lost because it was not in the owner's

purse, and a son who was lost because he was not in his father's house.

B. Man was created by God to enjoy a filial relationship with Him, but having created man in His image, God gave him the privilege of choosing. He did not want to create a robot. No one finds satisfaction in the obedience of subjection and slavery, but because one wills to obey. God knew that this kind of willing obedience was the ultimate happiness. Thus God gave man this initial opportunity, but he rejected it. He became lost to God and this intended state of bliss. Man in this state of disobedience and alienation is selfish. He does not consider an attitude or act of altruism as wise. His philosophy is: "Why die for my enemy? He chose to disobey, let him suffer the consequences of his own disobedience. It would be utter foolishness for me to die to rescue him." When, therefore, man in his fallen, selfish state thinks of the cross of Christ which is an entirely unselfish act, he thinks of it as foolishness.

C. Who then is lost?

　1. All who have not believed on the Lord Jesus Christ and allowed Him through the shedding of His blood and death on the cross to save them are lost (Acts 4:12).

　2. The lost here stand clearly in contrast to the saved ones. If a person is not having fellowship with God as His child, then he is lost. If a person has never received Jesus Christ who died on the cross for his sins, then he is lost (John 1:12).

　3. Out of fear a person may perform certain religious acts, but that should never be mistaken as salvation. Salvation is the acceptance of what Christ did for each individual on the cross, not what the individual does to save himself.

D. The expression "to them that perish" in Greek is *toís apolluménois* which is in the present tense, a participial noun. The literal translation is "to them who are losing themselves."

    1. God must never be held responsible for one's lost estate. Man is responsible for his own lost condition.

    2. God never gives up on a man or woman. He is not put in the position of being hopelessly lost unless he dies without believing, "for it is appointed unto men once to die, but after this the judgment" (Heb. 9:27). God holds out open arms for each and every one to return at any moment while he still has breath.

IV. In Salvation There Is a Beginning but No Ending

A. The expression "unto us which are saved" in Greek is the participial noun *toís sōzoménois*, to the ones being saved. It is in the present tense meaning that there is a beginning and a continuing salvation. It is He who rescues us and He who keeps us. Salvation is in three tenses, the past: we have been saved from the guilt and penalty of sin (Rom. 5:1—were justified); the present: we are now saved from the power of sin (1 Cor. 15:1, 2); the future: we shall be saved from the presence of sin (Rom. 13:11). When the Lord saves us, He does not abandon us.

B. The tense is passive, we are being saved by Him. We don't save ourselves.

C. Paul included himself and all other believers who are saved and know they are, "but unto us." We should always be cognizant of our own individual salvation: ". . . for I know whom I have believed and am persuaded that he is able to keep that which I have committed unto him against that day" (2 Tim. 1:12), but we must never lose sight that the same salvation is the share of others also.

V. There Is Power in the Cross

A. The cross is considered a symbol of defeat by those who are lost. It seems to them that Christ died a helpless death on the cross. This is because they have never experienced the power that is in the blood of Christ to cleanse them from all sin (1 John 1:7).

B. Once a person experiences this *dúnamis*, power, he will not only know that the cross is not foolishness, but will not be ashamed of it. He will be proud of it as Paul was (Rom. 1:16).

How Wise Is God?

Key Verses: 1 Corinthians 2:6-13

I. Paul Declares That Believers Are the Wisest People Possible

    A. In 1 Corinthians 2:1–5 Paul told the Corinthian believers that he had not come to them in words of human wisdom.

    B. But in verse 2 he tells them that Him whom he declared to them, "Jesus Christ and him crucified," did not lack divine wisdom. "Howbeit we speak wisdom among them that are perfect: yet not the wisdom of this world . . ." (v. 6).

    C. He calls Jesus Christ "the wisdom of God," and what He did on the cross was the wisest thing possible. Christ is called "the power of God, and the wisdom of God" (1 Cor. 1:24).

    D. But He is not wisdom to all. To the Greeks He is a foolishness and to the Jews, a stumbling block.

    E. He is wisdom only to "them which are called" (effectively called, i.e., those who receive Him and became children of God [1 Cor. 1:24]). In 1 Corinthians 2:6 Paul calls them the "perfect" ones. The word "perfect" in Greek is *téleioi*, those who reached or attained the goal set by their creator for them. God did not create man to be an enemy of His, but to have fellowship with Him. But man chose to turn his back on God and became His enemy. The only way to reconcile man to God and to change him was through the sending of His Son into the world to become man and to give His life as a ransom for him (Rom. 5:11; 2 Cor. 5:18–20). The Greeks thought dying for one's enemies was foolishness. They considered that one does not die for his enemies, but being stronger as God must be, one eliminates them. The Jews expected a Messiah who would reign, not one who would suffer and die. But changing man to a friend from an enemy is far better than killing him. That takes not only power, but love (John 3:16; Rom. 1:16). But the only ones who would recognize the wisdom of the crucified Christ are the ones who permitted Him by faith to save them, to bring them to Himself. To the elect or "called" or the "perfect" (1 Cor. 1:24, 26), "Jesus Christ and him crucified" (2:2) is "wisdom of God." The only way for anyone to recognize the wisdom in God's action is to experience its transforming power.

II. The Wisdom of This Age Is Different from God's Wisdom

A. ". . . yet not the wisdom of this world" (1 Cor. 2:6). The word for "world" is *aiōn*, age, time period. The wisdom of this age is sinful.

B. Because it is not eternal, it takes into account only the here and now.

C. It is selfish. It is based on the survival of the fittest, instead of the stronger dying for the weaker.

D. It leaves God out of the picture.

E. It may feel sorry for those suffering but it cannot appropriate the suffering in order to bring an end to it and restore man to His original, intended state of being. A little boy asked, "Why is it that when I open a marigold it dies, but if God does it, it's so beautiful?" Before anyone could answer him, he said, "I know! It's because God always works from the inside out."

III. God's Wisdom Is Not the Same as That of the Wisdom of the Rulers of This Age

A. Those who rule do not place those whom they rule above their own selfish interests, but God so loved that He gave His Son to die for us while we were His enemies (John 15:13; Rom. 5:7). Man would love to make his enemies his friends or servants, but that is often impossible. However, God, through the power of the cross, can save a soul and cause him to dedicate his life totally to Him. One must experience the power of the cross in order to admit its wisdom (Rom. 1:16). This power must precede its wisdom (1 Cor. 1:24). Jesus Christ was "declared to be the Son of God with power" (Rom. 1:4; 1 Cor. 1:18; 2:4, 5; 4:20).

B. Those who rule us in this world cannot prepare us for eternity, but God gives us eternal life, a quality life for the here-and-now and a blissful life for eternity. It takes God to do this. Christ said, ". . . that in me ye might have peace. In the world ye shall have tribulation, but be of good cheer: I have overcome the world" (John 16:33. See 1 Corinthians 15:26, 54, 55). "If in this life only we have hope in Christ we are of all men most miserable" (1 Cor. 15:19; also Phil. 1:21; 3:21).

C. The Christian must realize that those who rule over them are not the real rulers, but are only acting as such. They are called *árchontes*, rulers, the present participle of *árchō*, while Christ is spoken of as the *archēgós*, "the prince," or the inherent leader, the source, the author, the cause of life (Acts 3:15; 5:31; Heb. 2:10; 12:2). Those of this age are simply *árchontes*, those temporarily ruling over us, but always under God, the absolute Ruler and Sovereign. Their rule is being canceled out as time goes on. The verbal phrase translated "that come to nought" is *tōn katagouménōn*, who are being rendered inoperative. God is going to eliminate them one day and prevail as the only ruler (1 Cor. 15:24–28).

IV. **Through His Cross, Jesus Christ Has Shown Us That He Is the Resurrection and the Life (John 11:25)**

A. Had He not chosen to die, He would not have risen from the dead, thus becoming the firstborn from the dead (Col. 1:18). If through His cross He could demonstrate to us that we, too, shall rise (John 5:25), that constitutes the greatest wisdom that God could demonstrate to us.

B. What man has the power to rise from the dead to demonstrate how wise he is? He who defeated death has to be acknowledged as having wisdom greater than the corporate wisdom of all humans during the ages.

The Glory of the Old and New Testaments

Key Verses: 2 Corinthians 3:12—4:2

I. **Confirmation of the Event in Exodus 34**
  A. God revealed Himself to Moses on Mt. Sinai (Ex. 34:5).
   1. He declared that the people were sinful and needed forgiveness (Ex. 34:9).
     a) In spite of Israel being God's chosen people, they were not exempt from the need of forgiveness (Rom. 3:23).
     b) No one is exempt from being heir to Adam's sin (Rom. 5:12).
   2. Their altars and their images had to first be destroyed (Ex. 34:13). The true God of Israel could not share His glory with man-made gods (Ex. 34:14–17).
  B. God delivered His commandments to Moses in writing on two tablets.
   1. This made possible the preservation of God's precepts.
   2. Moses' face caught the radiance of God (Ex. 34:29, 30).
   3. The radiance was proof of the genuineness of the commandments.
  C. No preacher who does not radiate God's glory can claim to be a genuine messenger of God's covenants.
   1. The disciples of Jesus were discerned as having been with Jesus.
   2. God writes His commandments in human hearts (2 Cor. 3:3) and unless His commandments are in

our hearts, it is better that they are not in our mouths.

D. When Moses faced Aaron and the people, he put a veil over his face because the glory of the Lord was a source of fear for them (Ex. 34:30–33).

1. God would not speak directly with the people, for they had sinned.

2. Moses acted as an intermediary even as Jesus was going to become a mediator between God and man (1 Tim. 2:5).

3. As Moses put a veil over his face to shield God's glory from man's sinfulness and man from God's holiness and glory, so Jesus Christ took upon Himself a veil of human flesh (John 1:1, 14) so that man might behold His glory as the glory of the only begotten or the unique One beside the Father (John 1:14).

4. Thus, God became approachable by the sinner because of what Christ did for man through standing in veiled glory between a holy God and sinful man.

E. Just as Moses in speaking with God did not need a veil, so Jesus is the only intermediary between God and man who, in His communication with the Father, needs nothing to hide God's glory from Himself.

II. Jesus Is Superior to Moses

A. Moses never made possible direct communication between man and God, but Jesus did.

1. We now have confidence (*pepoíthēsin*, from *peíthō*, to persuade) through Christ toward God (2 Cor. 3:4).

a) We do not need to approach God through any intermediary, but can come directly into His presence because of Christ and what He did, which caused the veil of the temple to be torn from top to bottom (Matt. 27:51; Mark 15:38; Luke 23:45).

> *b*) Because of the death and resurrection of Christ we have free access to God.

2. We should never pride ourselves on our free access to God, remembering that what we have is of God—He took the initiative to establish our direct contact with Him (2 Cor. 3:5).

3. Rather than a written law, there is a living relationship between the believer in Christ and God since He created in us a new life, which intuitively knows His expectation of us (2 Cor. 3:6).

4. He has made us adequate (*hikánōsen, hikanós*, sufficient, adequate) ministers (*diakónous*, deacons) for a new testament (2 Cor. 3:6). The word for "new" is not *néas*, which means simply numerically another testament or covenant, but *kainḗs*, qualitatively another one which gives free access to God's presence.

B. Compare Moses' and Christ's ministries and mediations.

1. Moses' ministry was unto death, for the letter (commandments on tablets) kills—prescribes the punishment of sin as death.

2. But Christ's ministry was unto life eternal, the life of God which never ends.

3. Moses' ministry was an indirect shining forth of God's glory (*dóxa*, from *dokéō*, to recognize). His mediation was to be done away (2 Cor. 3:8, 13).

4. But Christ's mediation was of righteousness (*dikaiosúnē*), transferring the right (*dikaíōma*) of free access to redeemed man.

III. **An Unsaved Person Is Still Unable to See God's Glory, to Recognize Who God Is, Unless He Receives Jesus Christ as His Lord and Savior**

A. The Old Testament is not an end in itself. It was merely the shadow leading to the substance (Heb. 8:5; 10:1), the New Testament.

B. The veil still exists in an unbeliever who has a seared conscience and a dull understanding (2 Cor. 3:14).

C. When one comes to the Lord Jesus, the veil is taken away. He takes it away; we cannot do it ourselves (2 Cor. 3:16).

D. When the Lord is master of the human heart, than that redeemed heart is free, not bound. The binding of the heart by Christ to Himself allows Him to act and live freely in man. The more one is bound to Christ the more free he or she is to do God's will (2 Cor. 3:17).

The Trinity

Key Verses: 2 Corinthians 13:5–14

I. Paul's Benediction Affirms the Trinity of God

A. "The grace of the Lord Jesus Christ, and the love of God, and the communion of the Holy Ghost, be with you all. Amen" (2 Cor. 13:14). This closing statement in Paul's letter to the Corinthians is not dogmatic, but rather indicates an accepted, uncontested belief in a Triune God.

B. Paul's benediction mentions three spiritual blessings: grace, love, and fellowship, whose source is given not as one person, but three: the Lord Jesus Christ; **the** God (in Greek *Theoú* has the definite article in front of it making it refer to "the Father"); and the Holy Spirit.

II. Paul Invokes the Father and the Son and Concludes with Father, Son and Holy Spirit

A. Second Corinthians begins with prayer: "Grace be to you, and peace, from God our Father, and from the Lord Jesus Christ" (2 Cor. 1:2). Both of these blessings can only come from God, who is infinite and whose essence is spirit (John 4:24). The word *Theoú*, "God," has no definite article, which means that it refers to the Trinity as a whole. And then, as if to delineate who God is, he adds: "our Father and . . . Lord Jesus Christ." In other words, both are God and the source of the spiritual blessings of grace and peace. Grace is God's unmerited favor toward sinful man, and peace is the state of mind which follows appropriation of His grace.

B. Second Corinthians closes (13:14) with the three equal persons of the Godhead distributing three blessings: grace, procured by the shed blood of Jesus Christ; love, the acceptance by the Father of the ransomed sinner; and fellowship or communion between the justified sinner and God the Father and Son through the Holy Spirit (see John 16:13, 14).

III. **Paul Makes Other Allusions to the Truth of the Trinity**
   A. In 1 Corinthians 12:4–6 Paul states it is the same "Lord," "God," and "Spirit" that works through a variety of gifts.
   B. Romans 8:14–17, 26–30 says that "as many as are led by the Spirit of God, they are the sons of God" and that they are "joint heirs with Christ."
   C. In Ephesians 3:2–5 Paul refers to his own conversion in terms of the Trinity, and continues to refer to the three Persons in the Godhead.

IV. **Other Apostles Allude to the Trinity in the New Testament**
   A. Peter speaks of the Triune God in 1 Peter 1:2, 3–12, 17–22; 3:15–18; 4:13–19.
   B. In John's first epistle we find mention made in 5:4–8.
   C. Jude also refers to the Trinity in 1:20, 21.

V. **Christ Himself Verifies the Trinity**
   A. "Go ye therefore, and teach all nations, baptizing them in the name [observe it is one name, in the singular, indicating the oneness of the Trinity] of the Father, and of the Son, and of the Holy Ghost" (Matt. 28:19). In Jesus' final earthly command to His disciples, He also refers in a very natural manner to the three Persons of the Godhead: the "Father," the "Son," and the "Holy Ghost."

B. When Jesus tells His followers about the promised Holy Spirit, He refers to the Trinity in John 14:26: "But the Comforter, which is the Holy Ghost, whom the Father will send in my name, he shall teach you all things, and bring all things to your remembrance, whatsoever I have said unto you." He also speaks of the three Persons in John 14:16–31; 15:26; and 16:7–15.

C. If Christ were not God at the time He made these claims, then the Trinity would be just a hoax. No mere man would have invented the Trinity because it is beyond human reasoning and mathematically impossible. But that which we were unable to discover on our own, Jesus came to reveal to us.

D. The three terms, Father, Son, and Holy Spirit are not mutually exclusive, but are connected and correlated. Note that there is a free and natural interchange of the three terms, yet Scripture never adds a fourth term to the three upon the same footing.

VI. Despite the Clear Teaching of Scripture about the Trinity, There Is Still Only One God

A. We must never allow ourselves to drift into polytheism. Christianity is a monotheistic religion just as is Judaism (Deut. 6:4).

B. There is such a mutual interaction and fundamental unity among the three Persons that distinction amounting to separation is prevented from occurring. ". . . it is the Spirit that beareth witness, because the Spirit is truth" (1 John 5:6). The Holy Spirit is the witness with whom believers are indwelt (1 John 5:10). The writing (Bible) is ". . . the record that God [Father] gave of His Son" (1 John 5:10). As a result of the work of all three, believers have the warranty ". . . that ye may know ye have eternal life . . ." (1 John 5:13). It is clear that the one God is the witness. There are not three Gods, but one God!

The Humiliation and Exaltation of Jesus Christ

Key Verses: Philippians 2:1-11

I. **To Save Man, God Reached Down**
   A. To realize how greatly the Lord Jesus humbled Himself in coming to earth as a man, it is necessary to view the lofty height from which he descended.
   B. He flatly stated His equality with God the Father.
      1. "I and my Father are one [*hén*, not one person, but 'one in essence,' or 'equal']" (John 10:30).
      2. ". . . that ye may know, and believe, that the Father is in me, and I in Him" (John 10:38).
      3. "Who being in the form [*morphē*—inner essence] of God . . ." (Phil. 2:6). The verb *hupárchōn*, "being," means that which He was before He became man and that which He continued to be while He was incarnate. As the God-Man He was equal with the Father, but He chose to become a servant obedient unto death, which He voluntarily suffered for our sakes. If Jesus Christ was not what He claimed to be, He could never have accomplished our eternal redemption.

II. **Paul Urges His Followers to Emulate Christ's Humiliation**
   A. The theme of Philippians 2 is expressed in verse 3, ". . . in lowliness of mind [*tapeinophrosúnē*, 'humility'] let each esteem other better than themselves." And then in verse 5 he adds: "Let this mind be in you,

which was also in Christ Jesus." Verses 6–8 go on to describe Christ's humiliation. Of course, since we are not God, we can never humble ourselves to that degree. However, we can strive for a similar mindset.

B. To encourage us in this endeavor, Paul proceeds to present Christ's exaltation (Phil. 2:9–11). The "wherefore" of verse 9 connects Christ's glorified state with His previous humiliation.

III. **Because Christ Willingly Descended, God Subsequently Elevated Him to the Highest Position**

A. First Jesus "humbled Himself" (v. 8), and then God the Father (*ho Theós*, with the definite article indicating 'the Father') "highly exalted Him." In like manner, we should lower ourselves and let God lift us up.

B. God the Father restored to the Son of Man, as He liked to call Himself while on earth, "a name which is above every name," (Phil. 2:9). We are not told what that name is, only that it will be preeminent in heaven and earth.

C. In verses 10 and 11 Paul describes the worship of Christ by the believers of all ages.

1. "That at the name of Jesus every knee should bow, of things in heaven, and things in earth and things under the earth." The word "things" is not in the Greek; it is inserted. Actually the participial nouns refer to people, not things. All intelligent created beings will be included in these two categories, those who inhabit the heavens and the earth and the inhabitants of the present *hádes*, called *katachthónioi*, "those under the earth" (used only here).

2. "Every tongue should confess" (v. 11). The word *exomologḗsetai* should not be taken as indicating universal salvation. The word means "to bring out" (*éxō*) that which is agreed upon (*homologéō*, from *homoú*, "together" and *légō*, "speak"). The confession of the believers will be worship, but the confession

of the unbelievers will only be an intellectual acknowledgment on their part that Jesus really is the
Master and Lord. Their hearts will remain un-
changed and, therefore, condemned.

D. And all this adoration of both believers and unbelievers
will be "to the glory of God the Father" (v. 11). The
word glory, *dóxa*, means "acknowledgment" and implies recognition of the eternal relationship of Jesus
the Son, who humbled himself by coming into the
world to reveal God the Father (John 1:18).

How Can We Think as Christ Did?

Key Verses: Philippians 2:5-11

I. **Christ Provides a Perfect Model for Us**

   A. Christ had always existed in the form of God (Phil.
   2:6) even though He also took on human flesh (Phil.
   2:8).

   1. The word "form" is *morphḗ*, essential being, as contrasted to *schḗma*, fashion, used in verse 8: "And
   being found in fashion as a man." The first is the
   essence and the other is the external appearance.
   Jesus Christ had always been God, as indicated by
   the verb *hupárchōn*, showing continuation of His
   deity even when He became man (John 1:1; 14).
   Concerning His appearance in human fashion, however, the verb *heuretheís*, is used. "And being found
   in fashion as a man" (v. 8). What is translated "being
   found," *heuretheís*, is the aorist participle passive of
   heurískō, indicating the Lord in His incarnation as
   man had a beginning in time. In other words, He
   became for a time what He had not been previously.

   2. Man only exists for a short time in human form,
   and therefore, could never claim to be what Christ
   always had been, namely, God. He did not consider it robbery to claim equality with God because
   He always has been God.

   B. The preeminent characteristic of Jesus was His humility.

   1. While He was on earth He "thought it not robbery
   to be equal with God" (Phil. 2:6). Even as man,

Jesus had the authority to demonstrate His deity at all times, but He did not do so. His example teaches us that he who is great does not need to parade it before others who are of lower station.

2. "But He emptied Himself, having taken the form of a servant . . ." (v. 7). This is a more accurate translation. His emptying of Himself was an act of His own will. *Ekénōsen* is an active transitive verb in the aorist. At a point in history, He emptied Himself of that which He has always enjoyed "toward the God," *prós tón Theón* (John 1:1). This was the full recognition by the Father of His eternal Son. When He became incarnated He left that recognition behind. He was not going to find it on earth as the God-Man. John 1:18 declares that there was no time at which God the Father and God the Son as such were separated. The verb there is *ho ōn*, which means "who being" in the bosom of the Father. Because Jesus Christ had always been in the bosom of the Father (John 1:18), He had the full recognition or "glory," *dóxa*, of the Father. By placing Himself among men, He deprived Himself of this honor for the most part, only regaining it in full when He returned to the Father (John 17:5).

3. He took upon Himself "the form of a servant." The verb is *labōn*, the participial aorist active of *lambánō*, to take. This was not something placed upon Him; He was not forced to become a servant. Rather, He took the role upon Himself voluntarily by coming in the "likeness of men" (v. 7). Although He became flesh (John 1:14) and was truly man, yet in a sense He was only "in the likeness of man" because He was not sinful (Heb. 4:15). The reason for His death was not His own sin, but His voluntary assumption of our sin.

4. "He humbled himself, and became obedient unto death, even the death of the cross" (v. 8). Christ's humility was supremely demonstrated through His subjection to death on the cross. In this verse we do not have the two indicative verbs. Only "he humbled himself" is in the indicative aorist while "he became" is an aorist participle ("when he became" or "having become"). Our humility is shown when we are willing to die for Christ even as He died for us. His death, however, was redemptive for us, while ours for Him is a demonstration of our love. If we want to think as Christ did, we must not consider that we deserve any better treatment than that which Christ received.

II. The Greater Our Humility, the More We Are Honored by God

A. "Wherefore God also hath highly exalted him, and given him a name which is above every name" (v. 9). The verb *huperupsóō*, to lift up (more than any person would otherwise experience) is only used here. His elevation is the reward that Christ received for subjecting Himself to the cross. The climax of His glorification will occur when "at the name of Jesus every knee shall bow . . ." (v. 10).

B. In like manner, we, too, shall be raised and glorified with Him someday (Col. 3:1, 4) if we obey Him (Matt. 7:21) and maintain the humble mind of Christ (1 Cor. 2:16; Phil. 2:5, 6).

Who Are the Enemies of the Cross?

Key Verses: Philippians 3:17—4:1

I. **The Early Church Was Invaded by Many False Teachers**
   A. In Philippians 3:18 Paul uses the Greek word *polloí*, many, which he then designates as "enemies of the cross."
   B. Likewise, in His Olivet discourse our Lord admonishes, "And many false prophets shall rise, and shall deceive many" (Matt. 24:11).
   C. "False Christs" shall deceive by showing great signs and wonders (Matt. 24:24).

II. **We as Believers Are Told to Mark Them, Not to Follow Them**
   A. Paul does not hesitate to tell the Philippians to imitate him (Phil 3:17) just as he himself imitated Christ (1 Cor. 11:1).
   B. Believers are to discern whom to follow by this mark of humility or willingness to lose one's position (Phil. 2:3; 3:17).
   C. Paul emphasizes the importance of being alert by using *élegon*, kept telling you, the imperfect of *légō*, to speak. It was necessary for Paul to continually warn them.
   D. In Philippians 3:2, he calls such false teachers some strong names: dogs and evil workers, indicating that there is no room in the church for such as these.
   E. In fact, Paul feels so strongly about their deception that his indignation turns to tears "and now [I] tell you

137

even weeping. . . ." In Romans 16:17 Paul also says not only to mark false teachers (*skopéō*, to set one's attention on them) but even more importantly, to avoid them (*ekklínō*, get out of their way).

III. Health and Wealth Preachers Are Enemies of the Cross

A. In verse 19 Paul describes the enemies of the cross as people "who mind earthly things" and "whose God is their belly" (belly used here to represent concern for physical comfort).

B. Compare the false teacher's desire for ease with Paul's description of his own life of service in 2 Corinthians 11:27: "In weariness and painfulness, in watchings often, in hunger and thirst, in fasting often, in cold and nakedness."

C. Possessing wealth does not disqualify a person from Christian discipleship, but an undue emphasis on material prosperity will make him unfit.

D. The cross represents the supreme sacrifice which Christ made for our redemption. Those who evangelize with a message of comfort and ease are certainly far from the truth Christ revealed.

How Man Can Be Delivered from the Power of Darkness

Key Verses: Colossians 1:1–14

I. Introduction

A. This passage names the name of Jesus Christ three times. In verse 10, He is referred to as Lord. He must be both Savior and Master.

B. In verse 13, the relative pronoun "who" refers to Jesus Christ as having delivered believers from the power of darkness.

II. Our Deliverance Is an Accomplished Fact

A. He hath delivered us from the power of darkness. The verb translated "hath delivered" in Greek is *errúsato*, the aorist indicative middle of *rhúō* or *rhúomai*, to draw or snatch to oneself, to draw or snatch from danger, to rescue, to deliver.

B. The aorist indicates that this deliverance took place once-and-for-all at a particular time in the past. That was when Christ died on the cross. If He were not what He was, the incarnate God, He could not have done it. "Who can forgive sins but God only?" (Mark 2:7).

1. Observe how Paul stresses Christ's deity: "Who is the image of the invisible God . . ." (Col. 1:15). The fact that Christ could be seen, due to His incarnation, proved the reality of the invisible God.

2. "For in Him dwelleth all the fullness of the Godhead bodily" (Col. 2:9).

139

C. The middle voice indicates Christ drew upon Himself humanity's sins. Adam did sin as our representative. But Christ acted not only as our representative but also as our substitute (Rom. 5:12, 17, 18; 1 Cor. 15:3; 1 Tim. 2:6). He took upon Himself our sins and became sin for us (2 Cor. 5:21). Yet He did not become sinful. If He were sinful His sacrifice for us would not avail (Heb. 4:15), even as the sacrifices of the Old Testament (Heb. 10:4, 6, 8, 11) did not avail for once-and-for-all lifting the sins of the people. His sacrifice was once-and-for-all, and it delivered humanity from its sin, both inherited and personal. ". . . but now once [during the dispensation of grace] in the end of the world [upon the consummation of the ages] hath he appeared to put away sin by the sacrifice of himself . . . so Christ was once offered to bear the sins of many . . ." (Heb. 9:26, 28). He did it all. He never asked us. He did it because it was the only way whereby we could have available forgiveness of sins (Heb. 9:22). Jesus would have done this even if only one was to be saved. He took our sins and our diseases which are the consequences of our sin upon Himself (Is. 53; Matt. 8:17). He accomplished His work on the cross when He said, "It is finished" (John 19:30). The work He came to do was finished, but **He** was not finished. His work was effective because He delivered us from the power of darkness.

III. Christ Delivered Us

A. No one else could have done what Christ did because no one else was God-Man. He had to be what He was to do what He did.

B. Not only did He forgive us our sins as verse 14 says, but simultaneously He liberated us as individuals: "Who hath delivered **us**."

1. Christ does not only take away our sins which is the meaning of forgiveness, but also transfers us from the kingdom of darkness "into the kingdom of his dear Son."

2. Salvation is not a mere rescue operation but it is fellowship with Him who rescued us. We become His subjects and He becomes our King. The verb for "hath translated" in Greek is *metéstēsen*, the aorist indicative active of *methístēmi*, to transfer from one place to another. He did it on His own initiative. It is a fact of history. This is our positional salvation when Christ transfers us from darkness to light (Acts 26:18; Rom. 2:19; 2 Cor. 4:6; 6:14; Eph. 5:8, 11; 6:12; 1 Thess. 5:4, 5; 1 Pet. 2:9; 2 Pet. 2:17; 1 John 1:6; Jude 1:13). Darkness is the same as spiritual death, which characterizes the sinner (Eph. 2:1). He is given eternal life which is the life of God (John 17:2, 3). Those who receive this life are transferred by Him into the circle of Christ and thereafter they are said to be "in Christ" (1 Cor. 1:30; 3:1; 2 Cor. 5:17). Therefore, our deliverance is not only negative, from the power of darkness, but also positive, into Christ or into the kingdom of the Son of His love. To be in Christ is the ultimate of salvation.

C. We who are in Christ are not immune from the attacks of the Devil, evil people, or sin. But that love which brought us into Christ will never allow anyone to transfer us out of the circle of Christ. That would be defeat against Christ by Himself (John 10:28; 1 John 2:1).

1. Observe here how Jesus is called the Son of His love. This love not only rescues, but also keeps to the uttermost (Heb. 7:25).

2. This transfer is final, as the aorist tense of the verb *metéstēsen* indicates.

IV. **Who Are Actually Delivered from the Power of Darkness and Transferred to the Kingdom of God?**

A. Not everybody automatically is delivered from darkness.

1. God universally provides some things for all to enjoy whether they acknowledge God as the giver or not. These are the common benefits of His providence such as the air, rain, sun, physical life, etc.

2. There are, however, God's particular benefits and blessings that are only for those who acknowledge the giver before they can enjoy the gifts. Such are salvation and all its ensuing consequences. You can have peace toward God, be justified before Him, have access to and fellowship with God, rejoicing in tribulation, only if you by faith receive Jesus Christ as your Lord and Savior.

3. Observe how Paul prefaces his remarks to the Colossians in verse 4, "Since we heard of your faith in Christ Jesus. . . ." That is what you need for deliverance from the sower of darkness and for your transfer into the kingdom of the Son of His love. You need to repent (Mark 1:4; Luke 24:47; Acts 2:38) and to exercise faith (Acts 10:43; James 4:15). These are to be considered not as meritorious qualities, but as gifts of His love.

V. **What Is the Power of Darkness?**

A. Christ delivers us not only from the realm of darkness, death and sin, but also from the power of it.

B. The word for power here is *exousía*, which means authority. Once in Christ we are not under the authority of sin, although sin will take jabs at us. But it will never have mastery over us (Rom. 8:31–39). Fight us, yes, but not defeat us. We will lose a battle or two, yes, but not the war.

VI. Deliverance Continues

A. He who delivered us and transferred us told us to pray for and expect continued deliverance.

B. From whom or what are we delivered?

1. From the devil (Matt. 6:13; Luke 11:4) and any work emanating from him (2 Tim. 4:18).

2. From temptation (2 Pet. 2:9).

3. From the propensities of our dying and corruptible body (Rom. 7:24; 2 Cor. 1:10).

4. From our enemies (Luke 1:74) and evil people (Rom. 15:31; 2 Thess. 3:2).

5. From depression and defeat in suffering (2 Pet. 2:7).

6. From the mouth of a lion (2 Tim. 4:17), that is, impossible and overwhelming situations.

7. From persecutions of all kinds (2 Tim. 3:11).

8. From the coming wrath of God which is the Tribulation period (1 Thess. 1:10).

Are You Alive and Walking in a Steady and Orderly Fashion?

Key Verses: Colossians 2:6–15

I. Only Those Who Received Christ Have Life
   A. Man in his sinful condition is dead (Eph. 2:1). He cannot walk.
   B. He is Satan's, having obeyed him (John 8:44). He is estranged from God (Rom. 5:10; Col. 1:21).
   C. Man becomes alive unto God by receiving Christ (John 1:12; 3:16; Acts 16:31). Receiving Him is believing on His name; that He is the incarnate God (Col. 2:9) who became man to die for us (Col. 1:22).
   D. The verb which is translated "ye received" is not the basic verb *lambánō*, "receive, take," but the compound *paralambánō*, with the preposition *pará*, "from, beside." It denotes source and nearness. *Paralambánō* means to receive, from or to a short distance from the person or thing to be received (1 Cor. 11:23). In Colossians 2:6 as well as in Matthew 1:20; 2:13 where reference is to Joseph receiving his wife, Mary, and the baby, Jesus, it involves tenderness and responsibility. Even in the case of the devil taking (*paralambánei*) Jesus to tempt Him, we can understand a deceptive gentleness in order to make Him believe he was Jesus' friend who would help Him to bypass suffering.
      1. The idea in the verb *parelábete* in Colossians 2:6 is:
         a) You received Jesus Christ from God after you came near Jesus, felt His heartbeat and closely

observed His life, His words, His death, and His resurrection. Interestingly, that is the verb used in 1 Corinthians 15:1, 3, where Paul speaks of the Gospel which he received—*parélabon*, which the Corinthian believers received (*parelábete*, ye received). When it comes to delivering it to them, he again used the verb *parédōka* and not simply *édōka*, which indicates gentle delivery from proximity.

b) The gospel of Christ comes from God. He brings God to us and whatever God had for us He delivered them to us through Jesus becoming Emmanuel, God with or near us (Matt. 11:27; 20:23; John 5:36; 8:16, 18).

2. Received, *parelábete*, being in the active voice, involves an act of the human will. Neither Christ nor the Gospel is stamped upon us against our will. It is only by our receiving what God offers in Christ that we are born again, that we become saints (Col. 1:2).

3. *Parelábete*, being in the aorist, indicates that once faith was exercised by these believers, Christ became theirs and they became Christ's. It is an accomplished event. I place myself by faith in Christ, and then no one can snatch me out of His hands (John 10:28). If my faith is a pretension or a mere mental assent, He is the first one to know it and He will not include me in Him or baptize me into His body (1 Cor. 12:13) or seal me with His Holy Spirit. Ephesians 1:13 says in the Greek: ". . . in whom [Christ] when you believed [this is a genuine faith as ascertained by the Holy Spirit] you were sealed [*esphragísthēte*, aorist, once-and-for-all] with the Holy Spirit of promise."

II. The Full Title of Christ Jesus the Lord Is Used

A. Christ means the anointed one, the Messiah.

1. There are two elements in the Messiah. First, His priesthood, involved in His becoming our Savior through His death (Heb. 2:17; 3:1; 4:14, 15; 5:5; 6:20; 7:26–28; 8:1, 3; 9:7, 11, 25; 10:11). Second, His Kingship. He announced that through His Saviorhood, He would be King within man's heart (Luke 17:21). Later at the consummation of the age, it would come with visibility (Luke 17:20–37; Matt. 25:31–46). He had to be Priest-Savior first, and King-Ruler second. But the cross had to precede the Kingship. That was what His disciples and others could not understand, why one having inherent omnipotence ultimately to put all under His feet had to submit to the cross, forgetting that the cross became first the altar of the Priest and through it would become the throne of the King.

2. Christ is the first preeminent name of this unique Personality. He came down from heaven (John 3:13). If He had not come down from heaven, none of us could ever hope to get there.

B. Jesus was His human name, that which related Him to us.

1. It is of like meaning to the Hebrew common name of Joshua.

2. It was the name of the successor to Moses. When he was to become the leader, his name was changed from Hoshea to Joshua. The name Yahweh, Jehovah, was added to it so that Hoshea, salvation, became Joshua, the salvation of the Lord. The Greek transliteration of Joshua is "Jesus."

3. When Jesus was born, that was His heavenly ascribed name (Matt. 1:21). He became man to sacrifice Himself for us to bring us to God the Father, from whom He descended.

C. The Lord, *ho Kúrios*, is His supreme Name. It speaks of His being the Creator (Col. 1:16), the Sustainer of all things (Col. 1:17); the purpose and fulfillment of all creation (Col. 1:16), the Head of His church (Col. 1:18). He is Christ the Lord and Jesus the Lord in whatever form He chose to manifest Himself before His incarnation or after His incarnation as the God-Man or in His present or future manifestations. He is the Lord of all times.

III. **His Relationship to Us**
   A. He is our Savior-Priest. He intercedes for us, having redeemed us (1 Tim. 2:5; Heb. 8:6; 9:15; 12:24). For this relationship He deserves our faith.
   B. He is our Brother-man. For this relationship He deserves our love.
   C. He is our Lord. For this relationship He deserves our worship and obedience.

IV. **Our Responsibility to Walk in Him**
   A. Walking involves activity.
      1. It does not involve sleeping or passivity.
      2. It is a command in view of the misunderstanding that the Christian life may be conceived as inactivity.
   B. Walking is not flying.
      1. The Greek verb is *peripateíte*, made up from *perí*, around, and *patéō*, to tread with the feet. It is to move about, but with our feet on the ground. The Christian is a heavenly being living in the world of reality. It is not being so heavenly that one is of no earthly good. A Christian is one who by God's grace keeps heaven and earth in balance. He brings heaven to earth and leads earth to heaven. A Christian is not one who has exalted moments of visions of heaven and flies high, but one who makes heaven in him walk steadily on earth.

    2. There is yet another word for walk, *stoicheō*, used in Galatians 5:25; 6:16, and Philippians 3:16. It means to walk in an orderly fashion set by someone other than ourselves. And that other is the Holy Spirit, hence the more specific command in Galatians 5:25, "If we live in the Spirit, let us also walk [*stoichōmen*, walk in an orderly fashion as set out by the Holy Spirit] in the Spirit."

C. Walking involves direction and goal. It is not going in circles.

Keep Looking Up to Heaven

Key Verses: Colossians 3:1-11

I. **Why Look Up to Heaven?**

A. Christ rose from the dead.

    1. No doubt is cast upon that fact. Colossians 3:1 begins with a conditional conjunction, *ei*, which is not to be equated with *eán*, "if." *Ei* indicates a contingency as to which there is no doubt. It would have been better rendered "with," "accordingly," "since" or "based on the fact that you were raised together with Christ. . . ."

    2. The resurrection of Jesus Christ was absolutely established as a proven historical fact by Paul in 1 Corinthians 15. It was so proven by:

       a) The Scriptures—verse 4.

       b) His appearances for forty days after His resurrection—verses 5 and 7.

       c) Five hundred saw Him at once, which excludes the possibility of one or a small group having been mistaken—verse 6.

       d) The power of preaching depends upon this historical fact—verse 14.

       e) We who believe it and declare it would be false witnesses if it were not true—verse 15.

       f) Our faith would be in vain—verse 17.

B. Since Christ rose from the dead, then His death availed for our salvation.

    1. He died for our sins (1 Cor. 15:3).

    2. He rose for our justification (Rom. 4:25).

II. Christ Is Now Up in Heaven

A. His resurrection was followed by His ascension (Mark 16:19; Luke 24:51; Acts 1:9–11).

B. He is still there: ". . . above, where Christ sitteth on the right hand of God" (Col. 3:1), meaning the Father. Therefore, both the risen Christ and God the Father are now in heaven. Since Jesus was taken up into heaven (Acts 1:10, 11), then "up" is "heaven" and "heaven" is up.

C. Since we as believers at death go to be with Christ (Phil. 1:20–24) and since Christ is now up there, we go up to heaven where He is. This is gain, not loss (Phil. 1:21).

III. Christ's Physical Resurrection Gave Us Spiritual Resurrection

A. "Since, therefore, ye were raised together with Christ..." (Col. 3:1 according to the Greek).

B. The verb is *sunēgérthēte*, the aorist passive of *sunegeírō*, to raise together. The compound verb derives from *sún*, together, and *egeírō*, to cause to rise up.

   1. The verb *egeírō* means to raise or rise up from a horizontal position to an upright one. It may be used transitively, to raise up someone or something, and intransitively, *egeíromai*, to rise up. Another verb, *anístēmi*, to stand up, is used mostly intransitively in connection with the resurrection, from which comes the most common noun referring to the resurrection, *anástasis*. The noun form of the verb *egeírō*, *égersis*, a rousing, is used only once to indicate the resurrection of Christ (Matt. 27:53). But the verb *egeírō* often refers to Christ's physical resurrection as well as of others (Matt. 9:25; 10:8; 11:5; 14:2; 27:52, 63, 64; 28:6, 7, etc.).

   2. The Lord is going to resurrect our bodies (John 6:39, 40, 44, 54; Acts 4:2; 1 Cor. 15:21; 1 Thess.

4:14; 1 Pet. 1:3). Jesus spoke of "the children of God, being the children of the resurrection" (Luke 20:36).

C. In Colossians 3:1 reference is made to our spiritual resurrection as connected with the physical resurrection of Christ. Because He rose, we have spiritual life, having received Him (John 1:12) or having believed on Him (John 6:40). This spiritual resurrection is equivalent to "eternal life" or the life of God within the believer (John 17:2, 3). The resurrection of Jesus Christ is connected with our salvation (Phil. 3:10; Col. 3:1). Paul already had reminded the Colossians that their physical baptism was symbolic of their burial with Christ and that they were raised spiritually with Him (Col. 2:12).

D. The verb *sunēgérthēte* is in the passive voice, which indicates that this spiritual resurrection was the work of Christ upon our dead personalities (Eph. 2:1). We were raised together with Him potentially when He rose from the dead, and in actuality when we received Christ and were justified (Rom. 4:25; 8:33). Faith on our part (Col. 1:4, 23; 2:5, 7, 12) caused His resurrection to become our spiritual resurrection.

IV. How We Should Live

A. Not all those who have Christ's life within them enjoy Christ equally.

B. The measure of our enjoyment of Christ's life in us depends upon:

1. Where we have our eyes fixed, that is, down for what we can derive from earth, or up, how much of heaven we can enjoy on earth. "Seek those things which are above."

2. Is the Kingdom of God first or last (Matt. 6:33)?

   a) The verb seek is *zēteíte* in the present imperative active which means we are responsible for such activity in response to Christ's life in us, and we must seek it on a continuous basis. Our enjoyment of Christ's life in us is in proportion to how actively we live it.

b) In Matthew 7:7 our Lord told us: "Seek [*zēteíte*, exactly the same as in Col. 3:1] and ye shall find." The latter verb is *heurēsete*, in the future indicative active, which means we do not find everything that heaven has for us all at one time, but one thing at a time, and that finding is assured. Keep looking up, and one after the other you will find treasure after treasure of heaven, with which nothing on earth can compare.

c) In 1 Corinthians 14:12 Paul says, ". . . seek [*zēteíte*] that ye may excel to the edifying of the church." That can happen only as you keep looking up being zealous of spiritual gifts.

d) In 1 Thessalonians 2:6 Paul writes: "Nor of men seeking [*zētoúntes*, not sought, but seeking continuously] glory of men" (author's translation). Keep looking up from whence our victory is derived.

Grace Causes a Complete Turnabout

Key Verses: 1 Timothy 1:12-17

I. **Few Could Exceed Saul in His Opposition to Christ Prior to His Conversion**

A. In 1 Timothy 1:13 Paul calls himself a blasphemer (*blásphēmos* which is derived from *bláptō*, to harm, or *bláx*, stupid, and *phḗmē*, report). Either derivative fully describes Paul's activity before becoming a Christian, although he had been trained under one of the greatest religious teachers in Jerusalem, Gamaliel (Acts 5:34; 22:3). Paul showed his ignorance not only by rejecting Christ Himself, but also by attempting to arrest Christians and cast them into prison (Acts 9:1, 2). He was tireless in his purpose to defame Christ and His followers.

B. Paul next describes himself as a persecutor (*diṓktēs*, one who pursues others). Meaning to harass or maltreat, this particular Greek word is used only in 1 Timothy 1:13. Speaking about himself as an unbeliever, he wrote in Galatians 1:13: "For ye have heard of my conversation [conduct] in time past in the Jews' religion, how that beyond measure I persecuted the church of God and wasted it." The verb translated "wasted" is *epórthoun*, which means to destroy. In Acts 9:21, the same verb is used describing his persecution of the church in Jerusalem. Likewise, he kept the clothes of those who were stoning Stephen, the first Christian martyr (Acts 7:58).

C. Finally, in verse 13 Paul refers to himself as injurious (*hubristēn*, indicating a person who abuses his power). In Matthew 22:6, the verb form is used preceding murder. Thus, the progression of sin goes from giving evil report to actually harming those who represent good. Evil is never static.

II. But God's Mercy Reached Him

A. The miraculous conjunction "but" contrasts Paul's inexcusable behavior with God's inexplicable mercy.

B. "I obtained mercy" in Greek is *eleēthēn*, the second aorist passive of *eleeō*, to show mercy.

1. The verb form used indicates that God took the initiative in granting mercy (Acts 9:3–8).

2. God acted suddenly (Acts 22:6).

3. Jesus' call to Paul was accepted in a way that any man who is a stranger to Christ can believe and be saved (Acts 9:5, 6).

4. The mercy God showed Paul is irreversible (John 10:28, 29). We, likewise, are secure in Christ.

C. Mercy (*éleos*) is that miraculous power of Christ to eradicate or alleviate the consequences of our sin. God's mercy made it possible for Paul to be used by Him in spite of his terrible past.

D. The mercy of God became effective in Paul's life because he acted in ignorance and unbelief: "Because I did it ignorantly in unbelief" (v. 13). It is not so, however, for those who sin knowingly and willfully (Heb. 10:26).

III. The Grace of God Changed Paul (1 Tim. 1:14)

A. Whereas God's mercy deals with the consequence of sin, His grace actually changes the sinner in order to reconcile him in God.

B. Paul experienced not only God's mercy (v. 13) but also His grace, and in great abundance (v. 14). *Huper-pleonázō* means to superabound and occurs only here. There is enough grace for the worst sinner, and then a surplus.

C. God's grace affected two great changes in Paul's life: "faith and love." Can such a turnabout be seen in our lives?

Are You a Coward or Do You Have a Sound Mind?

Key Verses: 2 Timothy 1:1-14

I. Possessing a Spirit Is Peculiar to Man

    A. God gave a spirit exclusively to man at creation. The Hebrew word *nishmath* is translated "breath" in Genesis 2:7 and "spirit" in Job 26:4.

    B. At death, Ecclesiastes 12:7 tells us, "Then shall the dust return to the earth as it was: and the spirit shall return unto God who gave it." Thus when Jesus died, He gave up the spirit (*pneúma*; Matt. 27:50; Luke 23:46; John 19:30). Likewise at his death Stephen said, "Lord Jesus, receive my spirit" (Acts 7:59). When Jairus' daughter was revived, it was reported that her spirit returned to her (Luke 8:55).

    C. It is through our spirit that we can communicate with God.

        1. The believer, having been cleansed by Christ's blood, has access to God through the Holy Spirit, "The Spirit itself beareth witness with our spirit, that we are the children of God" (Rom. 8:16). The believer continues to worship by means of the spirit (John 4:23, 24). Christ is actually with our spirit (Gal. 6:18; 2 Tim. 4:22).

        2. The unbeliever, on the other hand, is separated from God by sin (Eph. 2:1) and, therefore, cannot perceive spiritual truth (1 Cor. 2:14).

II. Not All Believers, However, Demonstrate the Same Spiritual Sensitivity

A. There are Christians who are called *sarkikoí*, carnal, because of their spiritual immaturity. They follow men rather than God (1 Cor. 3:3).

B. Another sign of spiritual immaturity is fear. "For God hath not given us the spirit of fear . . ." (2 Tim. 1:7). The noun for fear, (*deilía*) occurs only in this passage and signifies cowardice. (The verb *deiliátō* occurs in John 14:27 and the adjective *deilós* in Matt. 8:26 and Rev. 21:8).

III. What Is a Spirit of Cowardice?

A. For the unbeliever it may be what hinders him from trusting Christ and His sufficiency. For example, the rich young ruler refused to follow Jesus because he was afraid to give up his comfortable life style for a less certain one. The tragic result of this reluctance is described in Revelation 21:8, "But the fearful [*deiloís*, cowards], and unbelieving, and the abominable, and murderers, and whoremongers, and sorcerers, and idolaters and all liars, shall have their part in the lake which burneth with fire and brimstone: which is the second death."

B. Believers, however, may also be affected by a spirit of timidity, fearing that if they seek God's kingdom and His righteousness first, the rest of life will pass them by. They lack the confidence in Jesus' promise that "all these things shall be added unto you" (Matt. 6:33).

IV. What Then Does God Give by Means of the Spirit (v. 7)?

A. First, Paul lists a spirit of power. The word used in Greek is *dúnamis*, the strength of accomplishment. By it we are able to achieve God's will.

B. Secondly, God gives a spirit of love, *agápē*, the ability to discern the needs of others and to meet them in the power of the Holy Spirit.

C. Lastly, Paul includes the spirit of a sound mind or *sōphronismós* which is derived from *sóos*, meaning healthy or saved (from which *sōtēría*, salvation, comes), and from *phrónimos*, prudent. The singular form, *phrēn*, means mind and the plural, *phrénes*. *Sōphronismós* literally signifies restraint or self-discipline. The adjective *sōphrōn*, then, would refer to a person who knows how to use his mind to apply restraints on his conduct as instructed by Paul in 1 Timothy 3:2 and Titus 1:8; 2:2, 5. Being of sound mind is actually the opposite of possessing a spirit of cowardice or timidity. Because of it we know when the Spirit of God within us wants us to go or when we should wait. Without such a spirit, we may be as useless to God as a car without brakes.

Is a Christian Exempt from Persecution and Suffering?

Key Verses: 2 Timothy 2:8-15

I. **Suffering Is Not Always Due to Personal Sin**
   A. All suffering is due to sin as introduced by Adam (Rom. 5:12).
   B. Creation at the beginning was made good, and free from pain (Gen. 1:31).
   C. When sin entered, suffering also entered in the form of conflict, pain, corruption, drudgery, and death (Gen. 3:15–19).
   D. In the new heaven and earth (*kainós*, qualitatively new, not simply another heaven and earth as ours is now) suffering will be finally abolished (Is. 65:17; Rev. 21:1, 4).
   E. The work of Christ is to ultimately deliver man from suffering, corruption and death (Rom. 8:21; 1 Cor. 15:26). This, which pertains to our bodies, will take place when we receive our resurrection bodies (Rom. 8:23; 1 Cor. 15:50–57) and there is a new concomitant environment in which such a body can live (Rom. 8:20–23; Rev. 21:1, 2). The salvation of our souls is immediate (Matt. 1:21; Rom. 8:23). Christ's death accomplished both the redemption of our souls, which is immediate, and the redemption of our bodies, which we have yet to realize (Is. 53; Matt. 8:17).
   F. Though Satan is regarded as having the power to make man suffer (Job 1:12, 2:6; 2 Cor. 12:7), they

suffer only in the hand of God, and it is God who controls and allows suffering (Is. 45:7; Amos 3:6; Matt. 26:39; Acts 2:23).

G. God set suffering as a necessary consequence of man's sin and so God can never be blamed for sin itself.

II. Did God Create Evil?

A. The evil He is said to have created (Ex. 4:11; Is. 45:7) in the form of sickness, calamities, physical deterioration, etc., was not a direct creation of God but only the resultant necessity of man's disobedience if man chose to disobey God. God neither planned nor directed man's fall, but He created the consequences that would result from man's obedience or disobedience. He could not have created the one and not the other. Failing to apply the consequence of man's disobedience would have proven Him unable to execute His declaration to man (Gen. 2:16, 17; 3:1, 3, 17–19). Thus the presence of evil, sickness, suffering, and death are proof of the trustworthiness of God's Word.

B. The restoration of man and the universe to their original creation is yet to come (Rom. 8:19–26).

C. But for now God follows a process we should be aware of so that we may not be confused.

　1. In His sovereignty, He tolerates evil in the universe, overruling it and using it to advantage in His administration of the world.

　2. He uses it to punish individual and national wickedness (Is. 45:7; Lam. 3:38; Amos 3:6). If He did not, there would be chaos. When men violate the basic laws of God, they experience the consequences of their actions which may be penal or retributive affliction (Matt. 9:2; 23:35; John 5:14; Acts 5:5; 13:11). God does not do this to get even with man, but His punishment is remedial, not only in view of those who experience suffering, but also in view of

the whole of mankind. How could God allow the suffering of many at the hands of a few, by doing nothing about all the evildoers in the world?

3. The Christian experiences suffering, trouble, and persecution as part of God's way of giving to His own the opportunity to grow spiritually (James 1:2–4; 1 Pet. 1:7). It is a chastening, not penal punishment. God would never permit it purposelessly (Rom. 8:28). It can never separate the true believers from God's love (Rom. 8:38, 39). It prepares the believer for glory (Rom. 8:18; 2 Cor. 4:16–18; Eph. 3:13; 2 Tim. 2:11, 12; Rev. 7:14).

III. How Paul Viewed His Suffering and Impending Violent Death at the Hands of Evil Men

A. This is all revealed in his last letter, Second Timothy.

1. ". . . I suffer trouble, as an evildoer, even unto bonds . . ." (2 Tim. 2:9).

2. There was an altruism about his sufferings: "Therefore, I endure all things for the elect's sake. . . ." (2:10).

B. There is never a hint in all of Paul's Epistles that His sufferings were unjust, or that he should have been exempt from them, or that they were caused by God because of His own personal sin.

C. He was a realist in that he admitted that from the human standpoint, sickness, persecution, and poverty naturally result in sorrow (2 Cor. 6:4–10; 11:23–33). His philosophy of suffering can be summarized in what he wrote to the Philippians: "For to me to live is Christ and to die is gain" (1:21). The Christian can never be a loser no matter what he goes through. The Apostle to the Hebrews expressed it well by saying: "Now no chastening for the present seems to be joyous, but grievous: nevertheless, afterward it yieldeth the peaceable fruit of righteousness unto them which are exercised thereby" (Heb. 12:11).

IV. The Secret of Victory in Suffering

A. "Remember that Jesus Christ of the seed of David was raised from the dead, according to my gospel" (2 Tim. 2:8).

   1. "Remember" in Greek is *mnēmóneue* from *mnḗmē* (only in 2 Pet. 1:15), which is the faculty of memory. *Mnēmoneúō* is a far stronger word than *hupomimnḗskō* in 2 Timothy 2:14, although they are both translated "remember" (v. 8) and "put them in remembrance" (v. 14). *Mnēmoneúō* is to make something a permanent part of one's faculty of memory. It is not something that one occasionally remembers.

     a) It is the present imperative which indicates continuity.

     b) The word is in the active voice which indicates that it is something that we must do for ourselves.

   2. The verb has a direct object, "Jesus Christ." The KJV has it periphrastically, "Remember that Jesus Christ of the seed of David was raised." It should be "make it part of your conscious memory" or "remember Jesus Christ." It is not "remember part of His life history," but "remember Him as a person, His whole history, the Word in the flesh, mocked, suffering, dying." He went through all that we His followers are going through (2 Cor. 1:5, 6; Phil. 1:29; 1 Pet. 1:21). Paul did not tell Timothy simply to remember Christ's resurrection, but also His sufferings which resulted in His glorious resurrection.

B. Observe Paul does not say "Christ Jesus" as he sometimes does (Rom. 3:24; 8:2, 39; 15:5; 1 Cor. 1:2, 30, etc.), but "Jesus Christ." Jesus was the human name of our Lord, and Christ, meaning the Anointed One, was His divine name. He who became flesh, man, human, suffered as such; His divinity conjoined to His humanity. Similarly the indwelling of Christ in the believer does not exempt him from the suffering which is part and parcel of our humanity.

C. To accentuate the stress of the humanity of our Lord, Paul adds "of the seed of David."

D. In verse 8 neither the passion of the cross nor the grave could defeat Jesus Christ. He rose from the dead.

E. Neither the KJV nor the NIV does justice in translating the perfect participle *egēgerménon* as "was raised" or "raised." The NASB has it correct: "risen." "Remember Jesus Christ risen from the dead." It is perfect middle passive, but middle in sense. Jesus Christ submitted to suffering and death, but He **raised Himself** from the dead. He suffered as Jesus: He raised Himself as Christ. And the perfect indicates that He is now alive. There is therefore no reason for we believers to fear suffering, sickness, or death. Make Jesus Christ, the risen One, part of your conscious faculty of memory.

The Inspiration of Scripture

Key Verses: 2 Timothy 3:14—4:5

I. Paul's Last Will and Testament to Timothy
A. Paul was to be tried and executed.
1. His main concern was not to prolong his life (2:9, 10).
2. His concern was that his son in the faith (2 Tim. 1:2; 2:1) do the following:
   a) Be not ashamed of the testimony of the Lord (2 Tim. 1:8);
   b) Be partaker with him in affliction; (also 2:3 with the basic verb *kakopáthēson*, endure hardness, suffer peril);
   c) Keep that which was committed to him (1:14);
   d) Be strong in the grace that is in Christ Jesus (2:1);
   e) Remember Jesus Christ (2:8; Greek text has Jesus Christ as the direct object of remember);
   f) Should show himself approved unto God . . . rightly dividing the Word of truth (2:15).
B. No matter what Paul was going to suffer, his belief was that ". . . the word of God is not bound," or cannot be bound (2 Tim. 2:9).

II. What Is the Word of God?
A. It is the message of God.
1. It was spoken to the prophets for transmission to the people (Ex. 20:1; 2 Sam. 24:11; 1 Kgs. 6:11; 12:22; 16:1, etc.).

2. It was also used to designate the special revelation of grace given in and by Jesus Christ (Luke 1:2; Acts 4:4)

3. It was the personal message of Jesus Christ (Matt. 13:20; Mark 2:2; 4:14).

B. It is the Bible, the Old and New Testaments.

1. Every word in the original writings was written by both men and God. God's Spirit guided the human authors not only in the expression of God's thoughts, but also the means, the words with which these thoughts were expressed. This is verbal inspiration of the Scriptures.

2. The Scriptures are also plenary inspired, which means that the verbal inspiration extends itself to every portion of the Bible.

3. It can then be said that each book of the Bible has both divine and human authorship with God speaking in man, God speaking by man (in his own characteristic linguistic style, but yet under the control of the Holy Spirit), God speaking as man, and God speaking for man.

III. Paul's Apologetic for Biblical Inspiration

A. His affirmation of inspiration is in 2 Timothy 3:16, a chapter that begins with a description about the prevalence of perilous times "in the last days" (2 Tim. 3:1). The present attacks on the verbal plenary inspiration of the Scriptures may be said to characterize ours as "the last days" of this present dispensation of grace.

B. Timothy is urged to: "continue thou in the things which thou has learned and been assured of knowing of whom thou has learned them" (2 Tim. 3:14).

1. Paul refers to himself as Timothy's teacher (2 Tim. 3:10). Not only does the teaching need to be right, but also the teacher. Today there are too many untrustworthy teachers of the trustworthy Word of

God. A teacher who is not truly born again and characterized by living faith in Christ should not handle God's Word.

2. What Timothy acquired, encompassed in the expression "which thou has learned," was not merely intellectual knowledge. In Greek the verb is *émathes*, the aorist of *manthánō*, to learn in such a way that your life is affected thereby. He learned from Paul, and that learning was trustworthy in that it led him to believe on the Lord Jesus.

3. What is translated as "hast been assured" in Greek is *epistṓthēs*, the aorist passive of *pistóomai*, which means "you were made believing." The verb *pistóomai*, which derives from *pistós*, a believer, and *pístis*, faith, occurs only here, and in this context must be interpreted as "to make one a believer," while *pisteúō* means to exercise faith, to believe, which may mean effectually believe or simply to intellectually be persuaded. Timothy, by what he was taught by Paul, did not simply learn, but he was made to believe and to exercise faith in what he was taught. This belief, of course, was energized by the Holy Spirit. Learning the Scriptures is not enough. It is the duty of the teacher to influence those taught to believe in the power of the Holy Spirit.

4. Only because Timothy became a believer did he recognize all that was in his teacher, Paul, a faithful servant of Christ. Faith recognizes faith (1 Cor. 2:11–16). This is what "knowing of whom thou has learned them" means, that is, you discern what kind of faith your teacher has—that it is not mere knowledge but saving faith.

C. Timothy learned the Holy Scriptures from infancy, but he was not saved until later when he was taught by Paul.

1. It is commendable to teach our children God's Word from infancy, but that in itself is not salvation (2 Tim. 2:15). It is a step toward salvation.

2. The Holy Scriptures actually are *tá hierá grámmata*, the holy letters. *Grámma* is a letter of the alphabet, a written letter (Gal. 6:11), anything written, an epistle (Acts 28:21; Gal. 6:11), a bill, note (Luke 16:6, 7), or writing such as a book (John 5:47). In 2 Timothy 3:15 it means the Scriptures of the Old Testament (see also John 7:15), since Timothy's mother and grandmother were Jews.

3. The Scriptures of the Old Testament must lead to salvation through faith in Christ Jesus.

   a) "Which are able" (3:15) is the participle *tá dunámena*, that is, which have in themselves the inherent power (Rom. 1:16) to cause one to recognize his or her relationship with God. The participle is in the present continuous: which have the power, not simply had the power in Timothy's case, but they can lead anyone to the saving knowledge of Christ.

   b) "To make thee wise" (v. 15) is *sophísai*, the aorist infinitive of *sophízō*, to make wise (*sophós*). *Sophós*, meaning wise, refers to the one who knows how to regulate his relationship with God, versus *phrónimos*, prudent, one who knows how to regulate his relationship with his fellow humans.

   c) "Unto salvation." The ultimate purpose of the study of God's Word is not to satisfy one's intellectual inquisitiveness, but to be saved from sin and be reconciled to God.

   d) "Through faith which is in Christ Jesus" (3:15). That is the only name by which men can be saved (Acts 4:12).

IV. **The Scriptures Make One Wise unto Salvation Because They Are Divinely Inspired**

    A. They could not lead to salvation if they were not inspired. Second Timothy 3:16 has no connection with verse 15; therefore it must constitute an exclamation implying this: The Word of God does what it does because it is what it is. If it were not God-inspired, it would not lead unto salvation.

    B. "**All** Scripture" is *pása*, meaning every part of it and all of it together. That is verbal plenary inspiration.

    C. No tradition should be accepted unless it is in full agreement with the written Word.

    D. "God-inspired," *theópneustos*, would be the correct translation with a passive meaning, "having been breathed out by God."

    E. Because it is God-breathed, it is also profitable, *ōphélimos*, beneficial:

        1. For teaching;

        2. For reproof, *élegchon*, conviction;

        3. For correction, *epanórthōsin*, causing one to stand upright again;

        4. For instruction, *paideían*, which means child training with discipline and chastening, "in righteousness" meaning that God's instruction with discipline for us as His children is always within God's right as our heavenly Father (Heb. 12:4–8).

What Should We Do When We Are Slandered?

Key Verses: 1 Peter 3:13-22

I. **The Believer Needs to Be Benevolent**
   A. "And who is he that will harm you, if ye be followers of that which is good?"
   B. We should be benevolent no matter what, and even if the good we do causes others to malign us.
   C. Our righteous deeds should not be done in the expectation of reciprocal kindness.
   D. The question as asked in 1 Peter 3:13 contains two possible expectations.
      1. In most of the cases, people will love us and be grateful for our goodness.
      2. In some exceptional cases, however, there will be someone who will malign us for having been benevolent. The verb "he that will harm you" in Greek is *ho kakōsōn*, the future participle of *kakóō* (also used in Acts 7:6, 19; 12:1; and 18:10). This verb denotes a single act of being harmed or hurt by another. Scripture warns us that despite our attempts to live a godly life, we may run into opposition from time to time.

II. **The Believer Is Blessed Who Suffers for Righteousness Sake**
   A. In 1 Peter 3:17, the important warning given is that the believer should suffer for his righteousness rather than as a result of his sin. We shall experience little of the presence of God if we merely reap what we have

sown. The blessing only comes when we suffer for our benevolence, not our wrongdoing.

B. As used in verse 14, the word *makárioi*, means to be blessed or indwelt by God. Because of the presence of Christ within us we can be made fully satisfied despite hardships. Matthew 5:10–12 also clearly shows that being *makárioi*, "blessed," may lead to suffering, but that this should in no way reduce one's joy in Christ. Conversely, persecution for the sake of righteousness actually increases such blessedness. That is why Peter advises the believer in verse 14 that he should not fear or be disturbed by people who hurt him because of his benevolence. Actually, the word "happy" of the KJV is exactly the opposite of what *makárioi*, means. The word "happy" in its Greek equivalent never occurs in the New Testament because it means satisfaction if all goes well for us. The Lord never promises us happiness in our circumstances but rather blessedness or inner peace in spite of what happens to us (John 16:33).

III. The Believer's Response in Suffering Is to Glorify God

A. Peter tells us that in the face of persecution, believers must sanctify the Lord. But God is already holy. In what way then can we sanctify Him? The answer can be found in the Lord's prayer, "Hallowed be thy name" (Matt. 6:9; Luke 11:2), which means to venerate as holy or not allow His Name to be spoken evil of. In fact, the Christian is especially observed to see how he behaves when he suffers unjustly. (It is to be noted that in the Lord's prayer the request is *hagiasthētō*, "let thy name be hallowed," an indirect imperative). Thus in times of persecution the Christian has a unique opportunity to glorify God before the watching world.

B. "Be ready always to give an answer to every man that asketh you a reason of the hope that is in you," Peter admonishes in verse 15. Suffering affords the believer a wonderful opportunity to tell of his hope in Christ.

1. One should avoid stressing, however, his own heroic stand in suffering. Such is self-glory.
2. Peter also advises in verse 15 to witness with "meekness and fear."
3. Verse 16 mentions "having a good conscience," which means that the believer knows his motivation and actions are pure before God, if not understood by men.
4. The final goal of the Christian is that by his style of life and patience in affliction, he will show his accusers to be false and God to be true (v. 16).

To Be Forewarned Is to Be Forearmed

Key Verses: 1 Peter 4:12-14

I. **Peter Warns Believers of the "Fiery Trial" Which Awaits Them (1 Pet. 4:12)**

A. Since the believers to whom Peter was writing in his first epistle were suffering for Christ's sake (1 Pet. 2:19, 20; 3:14, 17; 4:19; 5:10), he wanted them to know they were beloved, *agapētoí*, "ones deserving the love of God," in spite of their suffering. It is unfortunate that the NIV has translated *agapētoí* as only "dear friends" instead of "beloved" because it is essential that we remember as we suffer for Christ that we continue to be loved by God.

B. "Don't be surprised" is the correct translation of *mē xenízesthe*, which is a direct negative command. In Greek there are two negative particles, *mē* and *ou*. The first, used here, is subjective and the second is objective. *Mē* implies that one conceives or supposes a thing not to exist while *ou* expresses that it actually does not exist. The meaning here is "don't suppose that suffering does not exist in the Christian's life." The verb *xenízesthe*, "be surprised," is in the middle voice and means "do not permit yourself to be taken by surprise." It derives from *xénos*, "a stranger." In other words, sufferings due to one's association with Christ are not to be thought of as something strange. This suffering is real, but it is not strange! The verb is also in the present imperative, which indicates continuity. Peter wants us to have the attitude of constant

172

preparedness, and so that at no time shall we be surprised by any specific situation.

C. Peter follows the command, "don't be surprised" with the dative *tē̃ en humín purṓsei*, which indicates the cause of this surprise being "the firing, burning or conflagration, in you." First Peter 4:12 is the only place in the New Testament where the noun *púrōsis* is used figuratively. (It is used in its literal meaning, "burning," in Rev. 18:9, 18.) Here we do not have an external cause providing trial as in 1 Corinthians 3:13; 1 Peter 1:7; Jude 1:23, but rather we have the condition of the believer's being on fire in an emotional sense. Because the translators have rendered this phrase as "fiery trial" (KJV; "the fiery ordeal" NASB; "the painful trial" NIV), they have not conveyed the internal struggles faced by the believer undergoing persecution. Do we sometimes "burn up" or get "red hot" or "crazy mad" as we unjustly suffer trying to live holy lives? Such a reaction is only natural to the old man within us. Even the Lord in His humanity looked with anger upon those who accused Him for having healed a withered hand on the Sabbath (Mark 3:5). Peter then reminds believers to be prepared for such "red hot" emotions within themselves.

D. To complete the interpretation of this verse, note that the present participle *ginoménē*, "taking place" or "coming as a reality," is in the feminine; agreeing not with the masculine *peirasmón*, "temptation," but with the feminine *púrōsis*, "burning." "Beloved, don't be surprised at the burning taking place in you [as you have fellowship with Christ's sufferings, v. 13]; or resulting from sufferings because of your association with Christ, unto temptation," *prós peirasmón*. Even though *peirasmós* may also mean trial or testing, the primary meaning of it is temptation, the situation where one is challenged to make one of two opposing choices.

When one is emotionally disturbed or burning inside, he is apt to make the wrong decision. In this case, he may lower his standards and compromise to alleviate suffering. This weakening of our resolve is the reason that Peter must warn us ahead of time of the dangers facing us.

II. Peter Urges Believers to Rejoice in Their Sufferings

A. Instead of suffering causing the believer distress, he should constantly rejoice, *chaírete*. The verb is in the present continuous tense meaning that this should be an ever-present attitude. The Christian can feel this way because he knows he is sharing in Christ's sufferings.

B. In the future, when the glory of Christ is revealed, then the believer will rejoice, *charḗte*, the aorist subjunctive passive. This joy will be very special, so much so that Peter describes it by using the present middle *agalliṓmenoi*, from *agalliáō*, "to leap, to dance." *Ágan* means "much," while *hállomai* means "to leap, to dance, to rejoice much with song and dance."

C. Such will be our joy in heaven. In fact, it will be proportionate to our suffering for Christ on earth as indicated by the word *kathó*, translated as "inasmuch" or "in proportion as." Seen in this light, the forewarned Christian can indeed rejoice even in his afflictions.

The Exaltation of Jesus

Key Verses: Revelation 5:11–14

I. **This Heavenly Scene Involves Myriads of Angels**
   A. In Revelation 5:11–14 an incalculable number of angels is pictured worshiping Christ: "ten thousand times ten thousand" plus "thousands of thousands."
   B. It was God's intention that they should do so: "And again, when he bringeth in the first-begotten into the world, he saith, And let all the angels of God worship him" (Heb. 1:6).
   C. These same angels who were described as "ministering" to the "heirs of salvation" (Heb. 1:14) are now singing to exalt the Lamb which was slain (Rev. 5:6) enthroned in Heaven as the lion of Judah (Rev. 5:5).

II. **Angels Are Mentioned as Ministering to Christ upon Other Important Occasions**
   A. They announced His birth and praised God for it (Luke 2:8–14).
   B. An angel strengthened Jesus in the garden of Gethsemane (Luke 22:43).
   C. Two angels witnessed to His resurrection (John 20:12, 13) and to His ascension (Acts 1:10, 11).
   D. When He re-entered His heavenly home, "he was seen of angels" (1 Tim. 3:16).
   E. They also desired to know of his work on earth (1 Pet. 1:12).
   F. Finally, angels will accompany our Lord in His triumphant reentry into this world (Matt. 25:31).

III. John's Vision Also Includes the Worship of Earthly Beings as Well as Heavenly Ones

A. This celebration is predicted by Paul in Ephesians 1:10: "That in the dispensation of the fullness of times he might gather together in one all things in Christ both which are in heaven and which are on earth; even in him."

B. It also fulfills his prophecy in 1 Corinthians 15:27, 28 that "all things shall be subdued unto him."

C. Note in Revelation 5:14 that it is the believers who worship Christ, "And the four and twenty elders fell down and worshiped him that liveth for ever and ever." The same are also mentioned worshiping Him in verses 11 and 12.

D. The rest of creation acknowledges Christ as Lord (v. 13).

E. Of which group will you be part? Will you give your life to Christ now and fall down in worship with the elders? Or will you wait to acknowledge Christ until it is too late and thus, be judged on your own merits?

The Eternal State

Key Verses: Revelation 21:10, 22–27

I. God Is Supreme

A. In the new Jerusalem the Kingdom of God has now become visible (Luke 17:20).

B. At the center of the new city is God in the Persons of the Father and Son (Rev. 21:22).

C. It is God who is the source of light and power in the new city (Rev. 21:23).

D. Replacing the temple, God Himself is the focus of worship and homage (Rev. 21:24).

E. There is no need of gates because nothing that defiles will come into God's presence (Rev. 21:25, 27); the unrighteous have already been banished to the lake of fire (Rev. 21:8).

II. The New Jerusalem Also Represents the Church

A. The New Jerusalem is described as a city "coming down from God out of heaven prepared as a bride adorned for her husband" (Rev. 21:2).

　1. The church is the gift of God the Father to His Son (John 10: 28, 29).

　2. The church is compared to a bride and as such it is to be a pure virgin (2 Cor. 11:2).

　3. Only in this holy state is the church fit for habitation with God (Rev. 21:27).

B. The New Jerusalem is a picture of what the church will be in the future.

　1. The church will center her attention wholly upon God, Who will be her source of light (Rev. 21:23).

2. Nothing will come between the church and her worship of God; no religious ceremonies will be necessary (Rev. 21:22).
3. Suffering and sin, symbolized as night, will be gone (Rev. 21:4, 25).

III. Who Will Be in the New Jerusalem?
A. Clearly only those whose names are written in the book of life will be there (Rev. 21:27). All others will be cast into the lake of fire (Rev. 20:15).
B. The Book of Life represents those who have put their trust in God for their salvation (John 6:47) and includes the redeemed of all ages: those of the Old Testament, of the ages up to the Rapture, and of the Tribulation saints. All others will be judged upon their own deeds (Rev. 20:12).
C. There is also a need to persevere in our faith until we are at last with the Lord (Rev. 3:5). "He that overcometh shall inherit all things; and I will be his God, and he shall be my son" (Rev. 21:7).

The Lamb's Book of Life

Key Verse: Revelation 21:27

I. Introduction
   A. In Revelation we have Christ's description of the past, the present and the future. Revelation 1:19 provides this summary. The future events are described in chapters 4—22. These chapters are divided into three sections:
      1. The tribulation in chapters 4—19 of which our Lord spoke in Matthew 24:21 and Mark 13:24 and which will be different from anything our universe has ever known.
      2. The millennium in chapter 20.
      3. The eternal state in 21:1 and 22:5.
   B. Revelation 21 deals with the establishment of a new heaven and a new earth. The word meaning "new" (v. 1) in Greek is *kainós*, which means qualitatively new. The new environment will be different from our present one and fit for our resurrected bodies (1 Cor. 15:51, 52; 1 Thess. 4:16, 17).
   C. Additionally, the New Jerusalem will be *kainē* (fem. of *kainós*), qualitatively new (v. 2). This is the Church that was already caught up by Jesus (1 Thess. 4:17) plus the saints of the tribulation period (Rev. 7:14). These tribulation saints are the ones who will refuse to bow down to the antichrist since their names were written in the book of life (Rev. 13:8).
   D. The New Jerusalem is identified as the bride, the Lamb's wife (Rev. 21:2, 9), which is the Church of the redeemed.

E. Revelation 21 ends with the followings words: "And there shall in no wise enter into it anything that defileth, neither whatsoever worketh abomination, or maketh a lie; but they which are written in the Lamb's book of life" (21:27).

II. What is the Book of Life?

A. The expression "the book of life" occurs a total of six times in the New Testament (Phil. 4:3; Rev. 3:5; 13:8; 17:8; 20:12, 15; 21:27).

B. Of these, the most expressive passage as to its meaning is Revelation 20:12, 15 where the Book of Life is distinguished from certain other books: "and the books were opened, and another book was opened, and another book was opened which is the Book of Life; and the dead were judged out of those things that were written in the books, according to their works . . . and whosoever was not found written in the Book of Life, was cast into the lake of fire."

1. There are books which record the believer's works which will constitute the basis of the judgment for his rewards.

2. The Book of Life is the book in which God writes the names of the redeemed at all times, and it is only when one's name is in that book that entrance into heaven is permitted.

3. Those whose names are not in the Book of Life are not admitted into heaven, being lost forever.

III. When Are the Names of the Redeemed Written in the Book of Life?

A. Observe that it is not we who register our names in this book, as we do on earth in entering this or the other place.

B. In Philippians 4:3 we read: "whose names are in the book of life." It does not say who wrote them. It implies, however, that their labors for the Lord resulted from their names being in the Book of Life.

C. Revelation 3:5: "He that overcometh the same shall be clothed in white raiment; and I will not blot out his name out of the book of life, but I will confess his name before my Father, and before his angels."

1. Here the negative statement does not imply the possibility that the Lord does blot out some names.

2. The Greek text has a double negative *ou mē*, suggesting impossibility, that is, no never. The Lord says that it is impossible for Him to erase from the Book of Life those names that He Himself wrote in it.

3. There are three things that are assured concerning the one who is a victor:

   a) He will be clothed in white clothes, so all will know of his victory;

   b) His name will not be erased from the Book of Life;

   c) Jesus will confess his name before His Father and His angels.

4. He who wrote the name in the book knew the person was genuinely saved and that he would be an overcomer. By parallelism, only He (Christ) who wrote it could also have the authority to erase it, if that were within the realm of possibility. However, the assurance is that He will not—no never.

D. Revelation 13:8 concerns itself with the tribulation saints who will not bow before the antichrist in contrast to those who bow and worship him (1 John 2:18, 22; 4:3; 2 John 1:7), that beast that rose up out of the sea (Rev. 13:1), the man of sin, the son of perdition (2 Thess. 2:3). "And all that dwell upon the earth shall worship him [the antichrist], whose names are not written in the book of life of the Lamb slain from the foundation of the world."

1. The verb "written" in Greek is *gégraptai*, the perfect passive of *gráphō*, to write. This means that the names of those who worship the antichrist have not been written in the Book of Life. The perfect indicates that these names were not written in the Book of Life and they never were in it.

2. The phrase "from the foundation of the world" in the KJV is ascribed to the Lamb slain. There would be no theological difficulty to accept it as referring to the "slain lamb." The Lamb of God was destined to be sacrificed for our sins before the foundation of the world. God in His omniscience knew, but did not determine man's fall; however, knowing it, He provided for our redemption. We believe, however, that although grammatically the phrase "from the foundation of the world" might refer to the Lamb slain, in view of Revelation 17:8 which clearly states that it is the names which were not written from the foundation of the world, the translators ought to have attributed the phrase "before the foundation of the world" in Revelation 13:8 to the verb "have not been written." In this case the verse should be translated: "And all who dwell upon the earth will worship him, those whose names have not been written before the foundation of the world in the book of life of the slain lamb."

E. Revelation 17:8 states the truth of Revelation 13:8 positively. As those who did bow before the antichrist did not have their names written in the book of life from the foundation of the world, so the names of those written in the Book of Life, *gégraptai*, have been written *apó katabolḗs kósmou*, from the foundation of the world. They were written by the omniscient Christ.

F. Now the question is: Can anyone cancel out Christ's writing of these names? Impossible, because if so,

Christ would be charged with faulty knowledge in writing their names in the first place.

G. This writing of the believers' names in the book of life is equivalent to the baptism in the Holy Spirit. When Jesus Christ sees the hypocrisy of a dead faith which is a mockery, He does not attach that person to His body, the Church. When He sees that the faith of an individual is genuine, He writes his name in the Book of Life and attaches that person to His body (1 Cor. 12:13).

H. The writing of the names of true believers in the book of life is also equivalent to the believers being sealed with the Holy Spirit unto the day of redemption. This is the redemption of the body mentioned in Romans 8:23. See Ephesians 1:13 and 4:30.

I. Revelation 21:27 provides the contrast between two groups of people, those who habitually live in sin and those whose names are written in the Lamb's Book of Life. "And there shall in no wise enter into it [this is the New Jerusalem with its eternal bliss] anything that defileth, neither whatsoever worketh abomination, or maketh a lie: but they which are written in the Lamb's book of life."

   1. That which is translated "anything that defileth" in Greek is *koinón*, an adjectival noun. It means anything that is common or not sacred, that is, wholly profane. The implication is that one cannot be totally unclean and have his name written in the Book of Life.

   2. "Neither whatsoever worketh abomination or maketh a life." The verb "worketh" in Greek is the participial noun *ho poión*, the one doing or working an abomination and a lie. This is a habitual performance of life. Again, such a person cannot have his or her name written in the Book of Life.

3. No one whose name is not in the Lamb's Book of Life can enter the eternal state of the blessed. Note that the verb "enter" *eisélthē*, in the aorist subjunctive, indicates a once and for all entrance.

The Lord's Return

Key Verse: Rev. 22:12

I. Christ Promises to Come Back

A. "And, behold, I come quickly . . ." (Rev. 22:12). This promise also occurs in Revelation 22:7, 20.

B. During His earthly life Christ explicitly promised His disciples He would come back for them. The verb in John 14:3 is exactly the same as in Revelation 22:7, 12, 20 (*érchomai*, I am coming). It is not the future indicative *eleúsomai*, which would involve a definitive, one-time, punctilious coming. He did not say "I shall come," but I am coming at any time and in more ways than one. The Lord never revealed exactly when He would return.

C. Nevertheless, the two angels who saw the Lord ascend into heaven in His resurrection body used the verb in the future indicative, *eleúsetai*, He shall come (Acts 1:11). The idea indicated by *érchomai*, I am coming, of Revelation 22:7, 12, 20 is that the Lord after His ascension will come in different ways and for different reasons, until His final coming. This is indicated by *eleúsetai* of Acts 1:11, predicted by the two angels, and finalized when He will come to reign with His saints forever on earth and in heaven (Rev. 20:4–6; 21:1–7, 9–21).

D. According to Paul in 1 Thessalonians 4:13–17, Jesus will first come back to take the resurrected dead and transformed living believers to be with Him.

E. Next, He will come to smite the nations assembled against Him in order to prepare the way for His millennial reign on earth (Rev. 19:11—20:6).

F. Jesus will make His final appearance referred to in Revelation 22 when He returns for the Last Judgment (Matt. 25:31–46).

II. Will It Be Quickly or Suddenly?

A. Three times in Revelation 22 the word *tachú* is used and translated "quickly" (vv. 7, 12, 20). "Suddenly" or "swiftly" would be a more accurate translation.

B. The Lord's return will not be immediate (as men consider time, 2 Pet. 3:8), but it will be sudden when it occurs (1 Cor. 15:52).

III. We Receive Certain Rewards and Retributions Now

A. The rewards accorded to believers are listed throughout Scripture (Gen. 15:1; Ps. 19:11; Prov. 11:18; Ecc. 4:9; Matt. 6:6, 18; and 1 Cor. 9:17, 18).

B. For the unbeliever, however, there is inherent retribution (2 Thess. 1:9). Living estranged from God is the greatest punishment man can inflict upon himself in both the present and the future. After Adam and Eve sinned, they "hid themselves from the presence of the Lord God" (Gen. 3:8).

IV. Christ Will Bring the Final Rewards and Retributions

A. The Greek word used for "reward" in Revelation 22:12 is *misthós*, which actually means a wage for work done. The Lord will reward us for everything we have done for Him in this life. It is not a bargained pay (Matt. 20:2) but rather a recompense that He decides upon according to His sovereign grace (Matt. 20:4, 7, 14).

B. The terrible retribution for unbelievers, on the other hand, will be denial of entry into the heavenly city and an eternity spent outside God's love in total depravity (Matt. 25:41, 46).

Index of Greek Words

This is an index of the transliterated Greek words used within the text of this book. Words are listed according to the order of the English alphabet.

Greek	English	Scripture	Page
adókimon	rejected	Rom. 1:28	81
agalliáō	to leap, dance		174
agalliṓmenoi see agalliáō		1 Pet. 4:13	174
ágan	much		174
agápē	love		158
agapētoí	beloved ones	1 Pet. 4:12	172
aiṓn	age, time, world	1 Cor. 2:6	121
aíretai	taken	Acts 8:33	61
aírōn	take	John 1:29	61, 62
aitéō	to beg (persistently)		31
aleíphō	to rub	Mark 6:13	16
aleípsantes	rubbing	James 5:14	16
alētheías	truth	John 16:13	69
alēthḗs	true	John 8:16	47

Index of Greek Words

amnós	lamb	John 1:29	60, 61
anagennáō	to give new birth	1 Pet. 1:3, 23	57
anagennḗsas	(aorist participle of *anagennáō*)	1 Pet. 1:3	58
anapaúesthe	to rest while laboring	Mark 6:31	19
anástasis	resurrection		150
anastḗsetai	to raise oneself	Luke 18:33	85
anexereúnēta	inscrutable	Rom. 11:33	104
anístēmi	to rise		85, 150
ánthrōpos	man	Luke 18:2	55
antí	in place of		99
antilambánomai	to receive in place of		99
apékrupsas	hid	Matt. 11:25	6
apeloúsathe	are washed		91
aphḗte	forgive	John 20:23	69, 70
aphíēmi	forgive		48, 70
aphíentai	are remitted	John 20:23	70
apó	from		6, 182
apokalúptō	revealed		6

188

apókruphai	hidden, unapproachable		6, 7
apokrúptō	to hide from		6
apolluménois	perishing ones	1 Cor. 1:18	118
apoloúō	to wash fully		91
apolúete	(imperative of *apoloúō*)		48
apolúō	to set loose from	Luke 6:37	48
apothaneín see *apothnḗskō*			94
apothnḗskein see *apothnḗskō*		Rom. 8:13	94, 97
apothnḗskō	to die off		94
apókrupha	hidden mysteries		7
apóstolos	apostle		16
archēgós	prince	Acts 3:15; 5:31; Heb. 2:10; 12:2	122
árchō	to rule		122
árchontes	rulers		122
arḗn	lamb	Luke 10:3	61
arníon	little lamb	John 21:15	61
astheneías	infirmities	Rom. 8:26	99

deilía	fear	2 Tim. 1:7	157
deiliátō	to fear	John 14:27	157
deiloís	(dative plural of *deilós*)	Rev. 21:8	157
deilós	fearful	Matt. 8:26; Rev. 21:8	157
deín	ought	Luke 18:1	52
diakaíōma	right		126
diakónous	deacons, servants	2 Cor. 3:6	126
dídōmi	to give		13, 105
diesteílato	to prohibit, forbid	Matt. 16:20	25
díkaion	right, just	Luke 12:57	47
dikaióō	to render just		92
dikaiosúnē	righteousness		126
dióktēs	one who pursues another, persecutor	1 Tim. 1:13	153
dokéō	to recognize		126
doulóō	to make a slave		89
doúlos	slave		89
dóxa	glory	Phil. 2:11	126, 133, 135
dunámena	able ones	2 Tim. 3:15	167

dúnamis	power; might	Rom. 1:16; 2 Tim. 1:7	119, 157
dunatós	mighty one	Luke 1:49	39
eán	if		2, 149
edikaiṓthēte	you are justified		92
édōka	give		145
edoulṓthēte	became servants	Rom. 6:18	89
egēgerménon	raised	2 Tim. 2:8	163
egeírantos	the one who raised		85
egeíras	raised one		85
egeírō	to raise up	(see text for references)	85, 150
egeíromai	to rise		85, 150
egéneto	became	John 1:14	60, 79
egeroúmai	will raise myself		85
égersis	a rousing		150
ēgérthē	raised	Rom. 6:4	85
égnō see *ginṓskō*		Rom. 11:34	104
egógguzon	were discontented, murmured	John 6:41	63
ei	if (suppositional)	Matt. 4:3, 6; Rom. 8:13; Col. 3:1	2, 94, 149

heuretheís	being found	Phil. 2:8	134
heurískō	to find		134
hierá	holy	2 Tim. 3:15	167
hikanós	sufficient		126
hikánōsen	adequate		126
hilasmós	propitiation	1 John 2:2; 4:10	114
hilastḗrion	propitiation	Rom. 3:25	115
ho	the (definite article)	(see text for references)	39, 52, 61, 62, 78, 84, 85, 114, 132, 147, 169, 183
hó	which (masculine nominative)		78
ho ṓn	who being	John 1:18	135
homoíōma	similitude	Rom. 8:3	79
homoiótēs	likeness, resemblance	Heb. 4:15	79
homoiōthḗnai	to be made like	Heb. 2:17	79
homologéō	to agree		132
homoú	together		132
hōsaútōs	likewise	Rom. 8:26	99
hósoi	as many, so many	Rom. 6:3	75
hubristḗn	an insolent person	1 Tim. 1:13	154

légō	to speak		52, 132, 137
lógos	word, the word	John 1:1, 14	52, 62, 79, 114, 115
loúsanti	washed	Rev. 1:5	91
–ma	suffix meaning result of action		111
makárioi	blessed ones	Matt. 5:10, 11; 1 Pet. 3:14	170
makarismón	blessedness	Rom. 4:6	73
manthánō	to learn		166
mathētḗs	disciple		16
mḗ	not	Luke 6:37; 18:2; 1 Pet. 4:12; Rev. 3:5	47, 54, 55, 56, 172, 181
méllete see *méllō*		Rom. 8:13	94
méllō	I will		94
metanoéō	repent	Mark 6:12	16
metéstēsen see *methístēmi*		Col. 1:13	141
methístēmi	to transfer		141
misthós	reward	Rev. 22:12	186
mnḗmē	remembrance	2 Pet. 1:15	162
mnēmóneue	to remember	2 Tim. 2:8	162

peripatoúsin	the walking ones	Rom. 8:1	77
phaneróō	to manifest		72
phḗmē	report		153
phílos	true friend		29
phóbos	fear		54
phoboúmenos	feared	Luke 18:2	54
phrḗn	mind		158
phrénes	(plural of *phrḗn*)		158
phrónēma	the mindset of man	Rom. 8:6	81, 82
phronéō	think		82
phrónēsis	thought process		81
phrónimos see *phrḗn*			158, 167
phronoúsin	think constantly	Rom. 8:5	82
pisteúō	to believe, to exercise faith		73, 166
pisteúontas	believing ones	Rom. 3:22	73
pistóomai	were believing		166
pístis	faith	2 Tim. 3:15	166
pistós	believer		166
pneúma	spirit	(see text for references)	69, 85, 87, 96, 156

Pneúmati	Spirit	Rom. 8:9, 11	92, 96
pneumatikón	spiritual	1 Cor. 12:1	111
poieí see *poiéō*		1 John 3:9	93
poiéō	to do, make		93
poión	he who does	Rev. 21:27	183
polloí	many	Phil. 3:18	137
prássō	to do	(see text for references)	95
práxeis	deeds	Rom. 8:13	95
pró	ahead		105
proédōken	to give ahead	Rom. 11:35	105
proētoímasen	to prepare before	Rom. 9:23	103
proetoimázō	to prepare ahead		103
prós	toward	1 Pet. 4:12	31, 135, 173
prosagōgḗ	access	Rom. 5:2	110
prosaítōn	one who begs	Mark 10:46; John 9:8	31
proseúchomai	to pray to God		100
proseuxómetha	pray	Rom. 8:26	100
psuchikós	natural man	1 Cor. 2:14	82

sophízō	to make wise		167
sophós	wise	Matt. 11:25	7, 167
sṓphrōn	applying restraints to one's mind	1 Tim. 3:2; Titus 1:8; 2:2, 5	158
sōphronismós	prudence, self-discipline	2 Tim. 1:7	158
sōtḗr	savior		106
sōtēría	salvation	Rom. 13:11	106, 158
sṓzō	to save		106
sōzoménois	saved ones	1 Cor. 1:18	118
splagchnízomai	have compassion		4
splágchnon	intestine, bowel		3
stenagmoís	groanings	Rom. 8:26	101
stoichéō	to walk	Gal. 6:16; Phil. 3:16	148
stoichṓmen see *stoichéō*		Gal. 5:25	148
stolaí	long clothing, robe	Mark 12:38	35
stolḗ	robe (masculine)		35
súmboulos	counselor	Rom. 11:34	104
sumphéron	to mutually profit	1 Cor. 12:7	112
sún	with, together		99, 100, 150

sunantilam-bánetai	to help	Rom. 8:26; Luke 10:40	99, 100
sunegeírō	to raise together		150
sunēgérthēte see *sunegeírō*		Col. 3:1	150, 151
sunetós	prudent	Matt. 11:25	7
tá	the (definite article, neuter plural)		167
tachú	quickly, suddenly	Rev. 22:7, 12, 20	186
tapeinophro-súnē	lowliness of mind, humility	Phil. 2:3	131
tḗ	the (definite article, dative singular)	Rom. 7:5; 1 Pet. 4:12	90, 173
tékna	children	Rom. 8:16	98
téleioi	perfect	1 Cor. 2:6	120
tḗs	of the (dative singular)	John 16:13	69
thanatoúte	to mortify	Rom. 8:13	95
Theón	God (accusative)	Luke 18:2; John 1:1	54, 135
theópneustos	God-inspired	2 Tim. 3:16	168
Theós	God (nominative)	John 1:1; Rom. 8:3; Phil. 2:9; Heb. 13:20	78, 84, 132

Scripture Index

1 Corinthians